HTC One (M8)™

FOR DUMMIES®

A Wiley Brand

HTC One (M8)™

FOR

DUMMIES®

A Wiley Brand

by Bill Hughes

FOR

DUMMIES®

A Wiley Brand

HTC One (M8)™ For Dummies®

Published by: **John Wiley & Sons, Inc.,** 111 River Street, Hoboken, NJ 07030-5774, www.wiley.com

Copyright © 2015 by John Wiley & Sons, Inc., Hoboken, New Jersey

Published simultaneously in Canada

For general information on our other products and services, please contact our Customer Care Department within the U.S. at 877-762-2974, outside the U.S. at 317-572-3993, or fax 317-572-4002. For technical support, please visit www.wiley.com/techsupport.

Wiley publishes in a variety of print and electronic formats and by print-on-demand. Some material included with standard print versions of this book may not be included in e-books or in print-on-demand. If this book refers to media such as a CD or DVD that is not included in the version you purchased, you may download this material at http://booksupport.wiley.com. For more information about Wiley products, visit www.wiley.com.

Library of Congress Control Number is available from the publisher.

ISBN 978-1-118-99286-9 (pbk); ISBN 978-1-118-99288-3 (ebk); ISBN 978-1-118-99287-6 (ebk)

Manufactured in the United States of America

10 9 8 7 6 5 4 3 2 1

Contents at a Glance

Table of Contents

Introduction

The HTC One (M8) is a powerful smartphone — certainly one of the most powerful phones ever sold. It's the flagship phone of HTC as of 2014, and supersedes the HTC One (M7). (From the rest of this chapter on, I refer to the HTC One (M8) simply as the *HTC One* unless it's important to make the distinction.)

Each cellular carrier offers a slightly customized version of the HTC One. Some cellular carriers come out of the box with applications, games, or files. Some come with accessories, such as a corded headset; others don't. This book doesn't dwell on these kinds of differences.

Although the name for each network is different, these phones are largely the same. (At least one marketing person at each cellular carrier is cringing as you read this.) This similarity allows me to write this book in a way that covers the common capabilities. At a more core level, this phone, regardless of the carrier, is built for high-speed wireless communications. The cellular carriers have spent kajillions upgrading their networks to offer more coverage and better data speeds than their competition. Again, this book doesn't dwell on these differences in network technology because they don't really make much difference. (Again, at least one engineering person at each cellular carrier is cringing as you read this.)

I assume that you already have a phone and that you have good coverage where you spend more of your time with your phone. If you don't have good coverage, you need to switch to another network; otherwise the experience with your phone will be frustrating. I suggest returning your phone to that carrier and buying your HTC One at another cellular carrier. Owning an HTC One will be an exciting experience, but only if you have good cellular data coverage!

First, in much the same way that different brands of PCs are all based on the Microsoft Windows operating system, all HTC One phones use the Google Android platform, regardless of the model or the carrier. The Android platform has proven to be widely popular — even more successful than Google originally expected when it first announced Android in November 2007. More people are using Android-based phones and more third parties are writing applications. This is good news because it means you have more applications options (more on this in Chapter 8 on the Play Store, where you buy applications).

In addition, all HTC One phones use a powerful graphics processor and a full HD touchscreen, and are covered in Corning's Gorilla Glass. The superior screen experience differentiates this product line from previous Android phones. Because of these enhanced capabilities, you can move around the screen with multi-touch gestures instead of using menus. Plus, the videos look stunning from many angles.

The HTC One comes with a "quick start" guide. And you can find lots of instructions on the web. And you've used a smartphone before. But you may not be familiar with a multi-touch screen, and your new phone offers a lot of capabilities that you may or may not be familiar with. It would be unfortunate to find out from a neighbor kid that the phone you've carried for months can solve a problem you have. However, you have to know what you *don't* know to get what you want. That's where this book comes in. This book is a hands-on guide to getting the most out of your HTC One.

About This Book

This book is a reference — you don't have to read it from beginning to end to get what you need. The information is clearly organized and easy to access. You don't need thick glasses and a pocket protector to understand this book. I help you figure out what you want to do — and then tell you how to do it in plain English.

I don't use many conventions in this book, but here are a few you should know about:

- Whenever I introduce a new term, I put it in *italics* and define it shortly thereafter (often in parentheses).
- I use **bold** to show something that you should type.
- I use icons in the margin to the left to help you find what you're looking for.

- I use `monofont` for web addresses and email addresses, so they stand out from the surrounding text. If you're reading this as an e-book, these links are live and clickable. *Note:* When this book was printed, some web addresses may have needed to break across two lines of text. If that happened, rest assured that we haven't put in any extra characters (such as hyphens) to indicate the break. So, when using one of these web addresses, just type in exactly what you see in this book, pretending that the line break doesn't exist.

Foolish Assumptions

You know what they say about assuming, so I don't do much of it in this book. But I do make a few assumptions about you:

- **You have an HTC One.** You may be thinking about buying an HTC One, but my money's on your already owning one. After all, getting your hands on the phone is the best part!

- **You're not totally new to cellphones.** You know that your HTC One is capable of doing more than the average cellphone.

- **You've used a computer.** You don't have to be an expert, but you know how to check your email and surf the web.

Icons Used in This Book

Throughout this book, I used *icons* (little pictures in the margin) to draw your attention to various types of information. Here's a key to what those icons mean:

Whenever you may do something that could cause a major headache, I warn you with the, er, Warning icon.

This book is a reference, which means you don't have to commit it to memory — there is no test at the end. But once in a while, I do tell you things that are so important that I think you should remember them, and when I do, I mark them with the Remember icon.

This whole book is like one big series of tips. When I share especially useful tips and tricks, I mark them with the Tip icon.

This indicates where you can go online to find more information.

You don't have to read these parts. I was kind of geeking out.

Beyond the Book

This book has more great online extras. To access the book's online cheat sheet, go to www.dummies.com/cheatsheet/htconem8. To read articles about the HTC One (M8), go to www.dummies.com/extras/htconem8.

Occasionally, we have updates to our technology books. If this book does have technical updates, they'll be posted at www.dummies.com/extras/htconem8.

Where to Go from Here

You don't have to read this book from cover to cover. You can skip around as you like. For example, if you need the basics on calling, texting, and emailing, turn to Part II. To discover more about photos, games, and apps, go to Part IV. To find out about the phone's calendar functions or about Google Voice, turn to Part V.

Many readers are somewhat familiar with smartphones, and won't need the basic information found in Parts I and II. A reasonably astute cellphone user can figure out how to use the phone, text, and data capabilities. Parts I and II are not for those readers. For them I recommend skipping ahead to the chapters in Parts III through VI.

Former iPhone users, on the other hand, are a special case. (Welcome to the world of Android!) The reality is that the iPhone and HTC One have very similar capabilities, but these functions are just done in slightly different ways and emphasize different approaches to the similar problems. iPhone users, don't worry if you find that this book spends a fair amount of time explaining capabilities with which you're familiar. You can read through those chapters quickly, focus on the *how* instead of the description of *what*, and bypass potential frustration.

Current HTC One (M7) owners are also a special case. The HTC One (M8) is very similar to the M7 in many ways. Both HTC One models operate mostly alike, but the M8 has improvements in usability, power consumption, and performance. If you're comfortable with the M7 and now have an M8, Chapters 15 and beyond would be of interest to you.

Part I

Getting Started with the HTC One

getting started

with the

HTC One

In this part . . .

- ✔ Review cellphone capabilities and what sets smartphones apart.
- ✔ Navigate your phone for the first time.
- ✔ Turn off your phone and manage sleep mode.
- ✔ Make sense of cellular billing.

Exploring What You Can Do with Your Phone

- -

In This Chapter

▶ Reviewing the basic capabilities of just about any cellphone

▶ Understanding what sets smartphones apart

▶ Mapping out what makes HTC Oncs so cool

- -

*W*hether you want just the basics from a phone (make and take phone calls, customize your ringtone, take some pictures, maybe use a Bluetooth headset) or you want your phone to be always by your side (a tool for multiple uses throughout your day), you can make that happen. In this chapter, I outline all the things your phone can do — from the basics, to what makes HTC One (M8) phones different from the rest. (From now on, I refer to the HTC One (M8) simply as the *IITC One* unless it's important to make the distinction from the previous version, which I call *Model 7* or *M7*.)

Throughout the remainder of the book, I walk you through the steps you take to get your phone doing what makes you the happiest.

Discovering the Basics of Your Phone

All cellphones on the market today include basic functions, and even some entry-level phones are a little more sophisticated. Of course, the HTC One has all the basic functions. In addition to making and taking calls (see Chapter 3) and sending and receiving texts (see Chapter 4), the HTC One sports the following basic features:

- **High-performance digital camera:** This resolution is more than enough for posting good, quality images on the Internet and even making 4 × 6 prints.

- **Ringtones:** You can choose custom ringtones that you download to your phone. You also can specify different rings for different numbers.

- **Bluetooth:** The HTC One supports stereo and standard Bluetooth devices. (See Chapter 3 for more on Bluetooth.)

- **High-resolution screen:** The HTC One offers one of the highest-resolution touchscreens on the market (1920 × 1080 pixels).

- **Touchscreen:** The HTC One offers a very slick touchscreen that's accurate, but not so sensitive that it's hard to manage.

Taking Your Phone to the Next Level: The Smartphone Features

In addition to the basic capabilities of any entry-level cellphone, the HTC One, which is based on the popular Android platform for mobile devices, has other smartphone capabilities:

- **Internet access:** Access websites through a web browser on your phone.

- **Photos:** The phone comes with a very intelligent camera, but it also can organize and edit photos.

- **Wireless email:** Send and receive email from your phone.

- **Multimedia:** Play music and videos on your phone with the best built-in speakers on the market. Or, you can plug in external speakers.

- **Contact Manager:** The HTC One lets you take shortcuts that save you from having to enter someone's ten-digit number each time you want to call or text a friend. In fact, the Contact Manager application, called "People," can track all the numbers that an individual might have, store an email address and photo for the person, and synchronize with the program you use for managing contacts on both your personal and work PCs!

- **Digital camcorder:** The HTC One comes with a built-in digital camcorder that records live video at a resolution that you can set up to and including full-HD.

✔ **Mapping and directions:** The HTC One uses the GPS (Global Positioning System) in your phone to tell you where you are, find local services that you need, tell you how good they are, and give you directions to where you want to go.

✔ **Business applications:** The HTC One can keep you productive managing documents while you're away from the office.

I go into each of these capabilities in greater detail in the following sections.

Internet access

Until a few years ago, the only way to access the Internet away from a desk was with a laptop. Smartphones are a great alternative to laptops because they're small, convenient, and ready to launch their web browsers right away.

Even more important, when you have a smartphone, you can access the Internet wherever you are — whether Wi-Fi is available or not.

The drawback to smartphones, however, is that their screen size is smaller than that of even the most basic laptop. On the HTC One, you can use the standard version of a website if you want. You can pinch and stretch your way to be able to read the information on the screen. (See Chapter 2 for more information on pinching and stretching. For more information on accessing the Internet from your HTC One, turn to Chapter 7.)

To make things a bit easier, many popular websites offer an easier-to-use app that you can download and install on your phone. This is discussed in detail in Chapter 8. Essentially, the website reformats the information from the site so that it's easier to read and get around on the mobile environment. Figure 1-1 compares a regular website with the app version of that website.

Photos

The photo app on your phone helps you use the digital camera on your HTC One to its full potential. (It would almost make sense to call the HTC One a smartcamera with a built-in cellphone!)

Studies have found that users of regular cellphones tend to snap a bunch of pictures within the first month of phone usage. After that, the photos sit on the phone (instead of being downloaded to a computer), and the picture-taking rate drops dramatically.

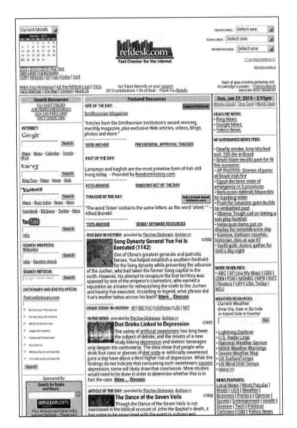 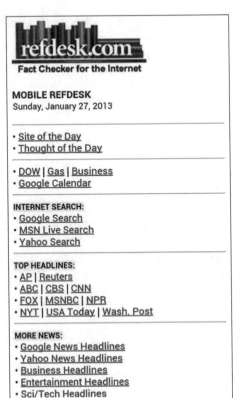

Figure 1-1: A website and the app version of the main site.

TIP

The HTC One image management application is different. You can integrate your camera images into your home photo library, as well as photo-sharing sites such as Picasa and Flickr, with minimal effort.

For more on how to use the photo applications, you can turn to Chapter 9.

Wireless email

On your HTC One, you can access your business and personal email accounts, reading and sending email messages on the go. Depending on your email system, you might be able to sync so that when you delete an email on your phone, the email is deleted on your computer at the same time. That way you don't have to read the same messages on your phone and your computer.

Chapter 5 covers setting up your business and personal email accounts.

Multimedia

Some smartphones allow you to play music and videos on your phone in place of a dedicated MP3 or video player. On the HTC One, you can use the applications that come with the phone, or you can download applications that offer these capabilities from the Play Store.

Chapter 12 covers how to use the multimedia services with your HTC One.

Business apps

Whether your company gives you an HTC One for work or you buy your HTC One yourself, you can use the HTC One to work with Microsoft Office applications.

Chapter 14 explores how to set up your phone to work with Microsoft Office applications (*apps* for short). After you set it up, you'll have unprecedented access to your calendar.

Customizing Your Phone with Games and Apps

Application developers — large and small — are working on the Android platform to offer a variety of apps and games for the HTC One. Compared to most of the other smartphone platforms, Google imposes fewer restrictions on application developers regarding what's allowable. This freedom to develop resonates with many developers — resulting in a bonanza of application development on this platform.

As of this writing, more than one million applications are available from Google's Play Store. For more information about downloading games and applications, turn to Chapter 8.

Downloading games

Chapter 10 of this book is for gamers. Although your phone comes with a few general-interest games, you can find a whole wide world of games for every skill and taste. In Chapter 10, I give you all the information you need to set up different gaming experiences. Whether you prefer standalone games or multiplayer games, you can set up your HTC One to get what you need.

Downloading apps

Your phone comes with some very nice apps, but these might not take you as far as you want to go. You might also have some special interests, such as philately or stargazing, that neither HTC nor your carrier felt would be of sufficient general interest to include on the phone. (Can you imagine?)

Your phone also comes with preloaded *widgets,* which are smaller apps that serve particular purposes, such as retrieving particular stock quotes or telling you how your phone's battery is feeling today. Widgets live on the extended Home screen and are available the instant you download them to your home screen.

Buying apps allows you to get additional capabilities quickly, easily, and inexpensively. Ultimately, these make your phone, which is already a reflection of who you are, even more personal.

Digging what's cool about Android

The HTC One is a top-of-the-line Android phone. That means you can run any app developed for an Android phone to its full capability. This is significant because one of the founding principles behind the Android platform is to create an environment where app developers can be as creative as possible without an oppressive organization dictating what can and cannot be sold (as long as it's within the law, of course). This creative elbow room has inspired many of the best app developers to go with Android first.

In addition, Android is designed to run multiple apps at once. Other smartphone platforms have added this capability, but Android is designed to let you jump quickly among the multiple apps that you're running — which makes your smartphone experience that much smoother.

Take a deep breath

You don't have to rush to use every feature of your HTC One the very first day you get it. Instead, pick one at a time. Digest it, enjoy it, and then tackle the next one.

I recommend starting with setting up your email and social accounts, but that's just me.

No matter how you tackle the process of setting up your HTC One, it'll take some time. If you try to cram it all in on the first day, you'll turn what should be fun into drudgery.

The good news is that you own the book that takes you through the process. You can do a chapter or two at a time.

You and Your Shadow: How Your Cellular Carrier Bills You

In the United States, most cellular companies sell phones at a significant discount when you sign up for a service agreement. And most cellular companies offer discounts on phones when you want to upgrade to something newer (as long as you also sign up for another couple of years of service). So, it's not surprising that most people buy their phones directly from cellular companies.

If your new HTC One device is an upgrade from an older phone, you might have a service plan that was suitable with your last phone but isn't so great anymore. If this is your first cellphone (ever, or with this particular carrier), you might start with an entry-level plan, thinking you wouldn't need "that many minutes," only to find that you and your phone are inseparable, and you need a better plan. The good news is that most cellular carriers allow you to change your service plan.

Most cellular service plans have three components of usage:

- ✔ Voice
- ✔ Text
- ✔ Data

I walk you through each of these components and how they affect using your HTC One in the following sections.

Voice usage

Voice usage is the most common, costly, and complex element of most service plans. Cellular providers typically offer plans with a certain number of anytime minutes and a certain number of night/weekend minutes. Some providers offer plans with reduced rates (or even free calls) to frequently called numbers, to other cellphones with the same cellular provider, or to other cellphones in general. If you talk a lot, you might be able to opt for an unlimited voice plan (for domestic calls only).

At its core, an HTC One device is, obviously, a phone. In the early days of smartphones, manufacturers were stung by the criticism that smartphones weren't as easy to use as traditional cellphones. Indeed, you do have to bring up the phone screen to make a call (more on making and receiving calls in Chapter 3). As an improvement, HTC has made sure that the screen used to make calls is only one click away from the Home screen.

If keeping track of minutes is important to you and your calling plan, be mindful of all those emails and social network updates that prompt you to call someone right away. You might be tempted to make more calls than you did with your old (dumb) cellular phone.

Text usage

A *texting bundle* is an add-on to your voice plan. Some service plans include unlimited texting; others offer a certain number of text messages for a flat rate. For example, maybe you pay an additional $5 per month to get 1,000 free text messages — meaning that you can send and receive a combined *total* of 1,000 messages per month. If you go over that limit, you pay a certain amount per message (usually more for text messages you send than those you receive).

As with voice, the HTC One makes texting very convenient, which in turn makes it more likely that you'll use this service and end up using more texts than you expect. However, nothing obligates you to buy a texting plan.

My advice is to get at least some texting capability, but be ready to decide if you want to pay for more or stay with a minimal plan and budget your texts.

Data usage

Texting may be optional, but Internet access is essential to get the full experience of your HTC One. The Internet, which is sometimes called *the cloud* (after the way it's symbolized in network diagrams), is where you access the capabilities that make the HTC One so special. Some cellular carriers may let you use the phone on their network without a data plan, but I cannot imagine why you'd want to do that.

Although your phone will supplement the coverage you get from your cellular carrier with Wi-Fi, you really need to have a data plan from your cellular carrier to get most of the value out of your investment in your phone. There's just no getting around it.

Most cellular companies price Internet access with usage increments measured in hundreds of megabytes (MB), but more often in gigabytes (GB).

✔ **Go for it:** Some cellular carriers make it easy by only offering unlimited data as an option. This is good news: As you customize your phone to keep up with your friends and access your favorite sites, the cost of access won't increase. There are no big surprises in store for people who choose this plan, even if it comes at an initially higher price.

✔ **Iffy:** Other carriers just offer very large "buckets" of data. In any case, it can be a challenge to figure out how much data you are going to need without going over the limit and paying a usage penalty. Some carriers try to help you by giving you some tools to estimate your usage by estimating the number of emails, web pages, or multimedia files you plan to download. These plans are a bit iffy. One option is to go with the lowest increment of data, unless you plan to be downloading a large number of videos. You can use some of the tools I cover later to see how much data you're actually using. Another school of thought is to go for an increment or two of data larger than what you think you'll need. After you've built up some history, you can call your carrier to scale back your usage if appropriate. An upgrade to the next bucket runs about $10 monthly.

Don't blame me if you don't check your usage and go over! It's easy to check and increase your usage, even mid-billing cycle. While the phone itself has some tools to measure your data usage, most carriers provide tools on the customer-service app they pre-load on your phone to track usage. I suggest you check this amount regularly. It is not an estimate. It is the official answer.

Another consideration: Family plans

A popular option is to combine your usage of voice, text, and data with that of your family members. The family unit on the plan gets to share a fixed allotment of voice minutes, texts, and data. This works well, as long as a responsible person checks your usage during the billing period!

Yet one more consideration: International usage

If you travel internationally with your HTC One, check with your carrier about your billing options *before* you travel. Voice and text usually aren't too bad when you roam internationally. Data is another story.

Rates for data when you're roaming internationally can be very high. You can end up with a very unpleasant situation if you don't check the rates and plan accordingly.

One final consideration: Web subscription fees

Don't forget that some web-based services charge subscription fees. WeatherBug (for example) offers a consumer service that gives you weather conditions, but it also offers WeatherBug Plus, which provides more information — with a monthly fee to subscribers and no ads. Yup, if you want WeatherBug Plus on your phone, you have to pay the piper. Some of these services can be billed through your cellular carrier (check first), but just make sure you're willing to pony up for the service.

What if I didn't get my phone from a cellular company?

With a few exceptions, such as an *unlocked* GSM phone, each phone is associated with a particular cellular company. (In this context, a *locked* phone can work only on its original carrier.) Maybe you bought a secondhand phone on eBay, or you got a phone from a friend who didn't want his anymore. If you didn't get your phone directly from a cellular provider, figure out which provider the phone is associated with and get a service plan from that company.

Some HTC Ones sold in the United States have the cellular company's logo on the phone. That makes it easy to know under which carrier a phone will operate. If there's no logo on the front, you'll have to figure out which cellular carrier it can work with. The quickest way is to take the phone to any cellular store; the folks there know how to figure it out.

To narrow down the possibilities on your own, you need to do some investigation. Take off the back of the phone to find the plate with the model and serial number for the phone. If you see IMEI on the plate, the phone is based on a technology called Global System for Mobile (GSM); it'll work with AT&T, T-Mobile, MetroPCS, or all of the former. If you see ESN on the plate, the phone will work with Verizon, Sprint, or U.S. Cellular.

Surviving Unboxing Day

When you turn on your phone the first time, it will ask you ten questions to set itself up. Frankly, they are trying to make this book unnecessary and put me out of business. The nerve!

The good folks at HTC are well intentioned, but not every customer who owns a HTC One knows, from day one, why they need another email account, whether he or she wants this thing called Dropbox, or what's a good name for the phone. You can relax. I'll help you answer these questions — or, when appropriate, refer you to the chapter in this book that helps you come up with your answer.

On the other hand, if your phone is already set up, you probably took a guess or skipped some questions. Maybe now you're rethinking some of your choices. No problem. You can go back and change any answer you gave and get your phone to behave the way you want.

The order of the questions varies by carrier, but includes the following:

✓ **Language/Accessibility:** This option lets you select your language. The default is English for phones sold within the United States. Also, the phone has some special capabilities for individuals with disabilities. If you have a disability and think you might benefit, take a look at these options.

✓ **Wi-Fi:** Your phone automatically starts scanning for a Wi-Fi connection. You can always use the cellular connection when you're in cellular coverage, but if there is a Wi-Fi connection available, your phone will try to use this first. It is probably cheaper and may be faster than the cellular.

At the same time, you may not want your phone to connect to the Wi-Fi access point with the best signal. It could be that the strongest signal is a fee-based service, whereas the next best signal is free. In any case, this page scans the available options and presents them to you. If you need to enter a password, you'll see the screen in Figure 1-2. If this is all too much to take in right now, feel free to skip to the next screen.

Figure 1-2: A pop-up window for a Wi-Fi password.

✓ **Date and Time:** This is easy. The default setting is to use the time and date that come from the cellular network. Just tap the next button and move on. This date and time from the cellular network is the most accurate information you'll get, and you don't need to do anything other than be within cellular coverage now and again.

✔ **Google Account Sign-up:** *Google account* means an email account where the address ends in @gmail.com. If you already have an account on Gmail, enter your user ID and password here.

If you don't have a Gmail account, I suggest waiting until you read Chapter 5. I highly recommend that you create a Gmail account, but it's best to go through some other steps first.

✔ **Location Options:** Your phone knowing your location and providing it to an app can be a sensitive issue.

If you're really worried about privacy and security, tap the green check marks on the screen and then tap the button that says Next. Selecting these options prevents apps from knowing where you are. (This choice also prevents you from getting directions and a large number of cool capabilities that are built into apps.) The only folks who'll know your location will be the 911 dispatchers if you dial them.

If you're worried about your security but want to take advantage of some of the cool capabilities built into your phone, tap the right arrow key to move forward.

You can choose on a case-by-case basis whether to share your location. (I cover this issue in Chapter 8.)

✔ **Phone Ownership:** This screen asks you to enter your first and last name. You may ask why this is important at this point. It's not. If you've been able to navigate this far, you may be ready to tap in your first and last name. If not, just tap the right arrow. All will be fine.

✔ **Dropbox:** This is a generous offer, but what is it for? (I explain Dropbox in more detail in Chapter 14.) You may or may not ever need this option. If you do, we can come back and take those folks up on this offer. For now, you can just tap Skip. Or, if you have a Dropbox account already, go ahead and enter your ID and password.

✔ **Learn about key features:** If you think you don't need this book, go ahead and take this tour of all the new things you can do. If you think you might need this book in any way, shape, or form, tap the Next button. This screen is for setting up the coolest and the most sophisticated capabilities of the phone. I cover many of them in the course of this book. For now, skip this to get to the last screen.

✔ **Device Name:** When this screen comes up, you'll see a text box that has the model name. You can keep this name or you can choose to personalize it a bit. For example, you can change it to Bill's HTC One or Indy at 425-555-1234. The purpose of this name is for connecting to a local data network, as when you're pairing with a Bluetooth device. If this last sentence made no sense to you, don't worry about it. Tap Finish. In a moment, you see the Home screen, as shown in Figure 1-3.

Figure 1-3: The Home screen for the HTC One.

2

Beginning at the Beginning

In This Chapter

▶ Turning on your phone

▶ Charging the phone and managing battery life

▶ Navigating your phone

▶ Turning off your phone and using sleep mode

In this chapter, I fill you in on the basics of using your new HTC One. You start by turning on your phone. (I told you I was covering the basics!) I guide you through charging your phone and getting the most out of your phone's battery. Stick with me for a basic tour of your phone's buttons and other features. Then I end by telling you how to turn off your phone or put it in "sleep" mode.

Unless you're new to cellphones in general — and smartphones in particular — you might want to skip this chapter. If the term *smartphone* is foreign to you, you probably haven't used one before, and reading this chapter won't hurt. And, just so you know, a *smartphone* is just a cellular phone on which you can download and run applications (apps) that are better than what comes preloaded on a phone right out of the box.

First Things First: Turning On Your Phone

When you open the box of your new phone, the packaging will present you with your phone, wrapped in plastic, readily accessible. If you haven't already, take the phone out of the plastic bag and remove any protective covering material on the screen.

There may be a plastic film on the screen. It would be nice, but it is not really an effective screen protector. Go ahead and take it off.

First things first. The Power button is on the top side of the phone towards the right side when the screen is facing towards you. You can see the placement of the button in Figure 2-1. Press the Power button for a second or two, and see if it vibrates and the screen lights up.

Hopefully, your phone arrived with enough electrical charge that you won't have to plug it in to an outlet right away. You can enjoy your new phone for the first day without having to charge it. The phones that you get at the stores of most cellular carriers usually come with the battery installed, partially charged, and registered with the network.

Power Button

Figure 2-1: The Power button.

If the screen does light up, don't hold the Power button too long, or the phone might turn off.

If the phone screen doesn't light up (rats!), you need to charge the battery. Here's the rub: It's important to fully charge the battery for 24 hours, or at least overnight, so that it will last as long as possible. That means that you have to wait to use your beautiful new phone. Sorry.

Playing with cards for the HTC One

To operate properly, your phone needs some cards that will be installed in slots on the side of your phone:

- ✓ Your SIM card
- ✓ A MicroSD card

As you can see in Figure 2-2, the SIM card is slightly smaller than the MicroSD card. The HTC One uses what is called a nano-SIM card.

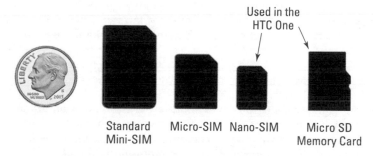

Used in the
HTC One

Standard
Mini-SIM   Micro-SIM Nano-SIM   Micro SD
Memory Card

Figure 2-2: Silhouettes of SIM cards and the MicroSD card.

While both cards are small, thin, and somewhat rectangular, they perform very different functions. The SIM card stores the information about your phone number. It also stores information so that the data network knows who you are.

You may have used a SIM card in the past. If so, you are familiar with the ability to pop out the SIM card, put it in another phone, and use the new phone to make and receive calls. Chances are that you used the standard mini-SIM. The nano-SIM can store more information, but is smaller.

The nano-SIM card is slightly smaller and thinner than the micro-SIM card and the mini-SIM card. Unfortunately you can't use a nano-SIM card with phones designed for the other formats, nor can you cut a micro-SIM card to fit. At best, trying to make it fit will not work. At worst, you could make it fit and it will probably break something.

If you aren't familiar with the benefit of SIM cards, now you get that benefit (although, why would you ever want to leave your wonderful HTC One?).

Total recall

The MicroSD card serves a purpose other than keeping your identity. You can use this memory card for storing files, music, photos, and video (more on this in Chapters 9 and 12). Let me jump in here to address a potential point of confusion: Your phone comes with built-in memory.

No, it doesn't just come with memory. It comes with a whole lot of memory. It can vary depending upon the model, but yours probably has 32 gigabytes of memory. This is huge!

However, this memory is built in and you can't remove it from your phone. The information stored on the built-in memory can be transmitted using a variety of methods I discuss in a number of later chapters. However, there are some files where it is just easier to pop out the card and insert it into another phone or a PC.

This scenario is where the removable MicroSD comes in.

When installed, you can have yet another big chunk of memory at your disposal. Your phone can handle up to 128 gigabytes of memory if you are willing to pay for a card this large! (I cover costs and sizing of the MicroSD card in Chapter 12.) This is mega-ultra–huge amount of memory!

Putting in and taking out the MicroSD card is easy once you've done it a few times. You may want to practice, but be careful not to lose the card. To remove a MicroSD card, follow these steps:

1. **Find the memory card slot on the right of the phone.**

   Figure 2-3 shows the location of the memory card slot and the tray ejection hole.

2. **Get the right tray ejection tool.**

   Figure 2-4 shows an official tray ejection tool option. You can get one for between $5 and $10 from selected retailers. The second option is a paper clip. It's available at many fine office supply stores in packages of 100 for somewhat less. Your choice.

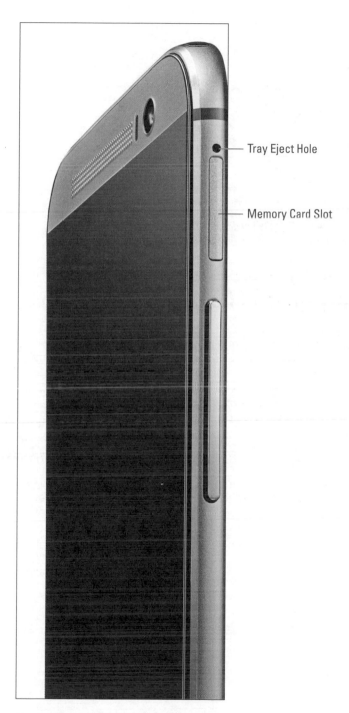

Tray Eject Hole

Memory Card Slot

Figure 2-3: The memory card slot on the HTC One.

Figure 2-4: The fancy tray ejection tool option for the HTC One. You can use a paper clip instead.

The nitty-gritty of how your phone works

As soon as you turn on your phone, several things happen. As the phone is powering up, it begins transmitting information to (and receiving information from) nearby cellular towers. The first information exchanged includes your phone's electronic serial number. Every cellphone has its own unique serial number built into the hardware of the phone; the serial number in current-generation cellphones can't be duplicated or used by any other phone.

The technical name of this electronic serial number depends on your cellular carrier. AT&T, T-Mobile, and MetroPCS call it an International Mobile Equipment Identity (IMEI) number. Verizon, Sprint, and US Cellular refer to it as an electronic serial number (ESN).

It doesn't matter to the phone or the cellular tower if you're near your home when you turn on your phone — and that's the joy of cellphones. All cellular networks have agreements that allow you to use cellular networks in other parts of the country and, sometimes, around the world.

That said, a call outside your cellular provider's own network may be expensive. Within the United States, many service plans allow you to pay the same rate if you use your phone anywhere in the United States to call anywhere in the United States. If you travel outside the United States, even to Canada, you might end up paying through the nose. Remember: Before you leave on a trip, check with your cellular carrier about your rates. Even if you travel internationally only a few times yearly, a different service plan may work better for you. Your cellular carrier can fill you in on your options.

3. **Insert your tray ejection tool into the opening and push until the memory tray pops out.**

   Your ejection tool will go into the hole and then hit something hard. Press firmly but gently and you will see the memory card frame come out a smidgen. Pull it the rest of the way out with your fingernail. The memory card rests loosely on the tray. It does not snap in to the tray, so be careful to hold the tray and card flat when you are inserting them into your phone.

Charging Your Phone and Managing Battery Life

Although you probably don't have to plug your phone into an outlet right away, here's a handy rule: The first time you do plug it in, allow it to charge overnight.

You'll hear all kinds of "battery lore" left over from earlier battery technologies. For example, lithium-ion (Li-ion) batteries don't have a "memory" (a bad thing for a battery) as nickel-cadmium (NiCad) batteries did. And the HTC One does use Li-ion batteries. That means that you don't have make sure the battery fully discharges before you recharge it.

Your phone comes with a two-piece battery charger (cable and the transformer), as shown in Figure 2-5.

Figure 2-5: The HTC transformer and USB cable for charging your phone.

The cable has two ends: one end that plugs into the phone, and the other that's a standard USB connector. The phone end is a small connector called a *micro USB* that is used on some recent HTC devices and is becoming the standard for charging cellphones and other small electronics — and for connecting them to computers.

To charge the phone, you have two choices:

✔ Plug the transformer into a wall socket and then plug the cable's USB plug into the USB receptacle in the transformer.

✔ Plug the USB on the cable into a USB port on your PC. See Figure 2-6

Then you plug the small end of the cable into the bottom of the phone. The USB is not rectangular. It's more a trapezoid, where one of the long sides is slightly smaller than the opposite. Be sure to position the plug correctly when you push it all the way in.

Micro USB Slot

Figure 2-6: The Micro USB slot on the bottom of your phone.

Unplug the transformer when you aren't charging your phone. A charger left plugged in will draw a small but continuous stream of power.

If your phone is Off when you're charging the battery, an image of a battery appears onscreen for a moment. The green portion of the battery indicates the amount of charge within the battery. You can get the image to reappear with a quick press of the Power button. This image tells you the status of the battery without your having to turn on the phone.

If your phone is On, you see a small battery icon at the top of the screen showing how much charge is in the phone's battery. When the battery in the phone is fully charged, it vibrates to let you know that it's done charging and that you should unplug the phone and charger.

It takes only a few hours to go from a dead battery to a fully charged battery. Other than the first time you charge the phone, you don't need to wait for the battery to be fully charged. You can partially recharge and run if you want.

In addition to the transformer and USB cable that come with the phone, you have other optional charging tools:

- **Travel USB charger:** If you already have a USB travel charger, you can leave the transformer at home. This accessory will run you about $15. You still need your cable, although any USB-to-micro USB cable should work.

- **Car charger:** You can buy a charger with a USB port that plugs into the power socket/cigarette lighter in a car. This is convenient if you spend a lot of time in your car. The list price is $30, but you can get a car charger for less at some online stores.

- **Photocell or fuel-cell charger:** Several companies make products that can charge your phone. Some of these products use photovoltaic cells to transform light into power. As long as there is a USB port (the female part of the USB), all you need is your cable. These chargers can cost from $40 to $100 on up.

Ideally, use HTC chargers, chargers from your carrier — or at least chargers from reputable manufacturers. The power specifications for USB ports are standardized. Reputable manufactures comply with these standards, but less reputable manufacturers might not. Cheap USB chargers physically fit the USB end of the cable that goes to your phone. However, Li-ion batteries are sensitive to voltage. If your phone detects something funny about your charger, your phone may notify you that it is limiting the charger to work more slowly. If you are in a hurry, you may want to get your HTC cable and transformer.

Li-ion batteries don't like extreme heat. If your phone is with you, and you can stand the heat, your battery will be fine. Also be aware that the conditions that make for a good charge also tend to make for high heat. It will do you little good to have a beautifully functioning charger and a dead battery.

If you take good care of it, your battery should last about two years, with a drop in performance of about 25 percent from pristine condition out of the box. At that point, you can replace the battery or upgrade to the newest Galaxy phone.

Navigating the HTC One

HTC One phone devices differ from other phones in design: They have significantly fewer hardware buttons (physical buttons on the phone). They rely much more heavily on software buttons that appear onscreen. In this section, I guide you through your phone's buttons.

The phone's hardware buttons

HTC has reduced the number of hardware buttons on the HTC One. There are only two: the Power button and the Volume button. Before you get too far into using your phone, orient yourself to be sure you're looking at the correct side of the phone.

Note: When I refer to the *left* or *right* of the phone, I'm assuming a vertical orientation (meaning you're not holding the phone sideways) and that you're looking at the phone's screen.

The Power button

The Power button is on top side of the phone, toward the right when you hold it in vertical orientation. In addition to powering up the phone, pressing the Power button puts the device into sleep mode if you press it for a moment while the phone is On.

Sleep mode shuts off the screen and suspends most running applications.

The phone automatically shuts off the screen after about 30 seconds of inactivity to save power, but you might want to do this manually when you put away your phone. The Super AMOLED (Active-Matrix Organic Light-Emitting Diode) screen on your HTC One is cool, but it also uses a lot of power.

Don't confuse a blank screen with powering off. Because the screen is the biggest user of power on your phone, having the screen go blank saves battery life. The phone is still alert to any incoming calls; when someone calls, the screen automatically lights up.

The Volume button (s)

Technically, there are two Volume buttons: one to increase the volume, and the other to lower it. Their location is shown in Figure 2-7.

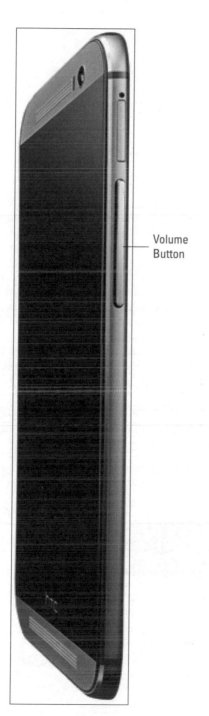

Volume
Button

Figure 2-7: The HTC One Volume buttons on the right.

The Volume buttons control the volume of all the audio sources on the phone, including

- ✔ The phone ringer for when a call comes in (ringtone)
- ✔ The "notifications" that occur only when you're not talking on the phone, such as the optional ping that lets you know you've received a text or email
- ✔ The phone headset when you're talking on the phone
- ✔ The volume from the digital music and video player (media)

The Volume controls are aware of the context; they can tell which volume you're changing. For example, if you're listening to music, adjusting volume raises or lowers the music volume but leaves the ringer and phone-earpiece volumes unchanged.

The Volume buttons are complementary to software settings you can make within the applications. For example, you can open the music-player software and turn up the volume on the appropriate screen. Then you can use the hardware buttons to turn down the volume, and you'll see the volume setting on the screen go down.

Another option is to go to a settings screen and set the volume levels for each scenario. Here's how to do that:

1. **From the Home screen, press the Volume key.**

   You can press it either up or down. Doing so brings up the screen shown in Figure 2-8.

   If you press the volume either up or down, the ringtone gets louder or softer. Let's hold off on this tweak for now, and go to the next step.

Figure 2-8: The ringer volume pop-up.

2. **From this screen, tap the settings icon.**

   The settings icon looks like a gear. It's to the right of the slider. Tapping it brings up the screen shown in Figure 2-9.

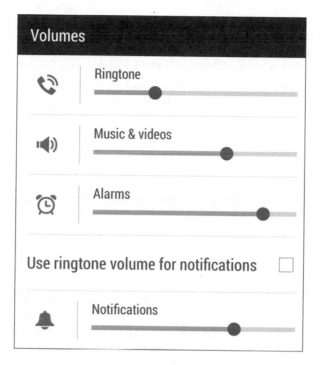

Figure 2-9: The Volumes settings.

3. From the screen in Figure 2-8, set the volume at the desired setting.

You can adjust the volume of any setting by placing your finger on the dot on the slider image. The dot will get bigger; you can slide it to the left to lower this particular volume setting or to the right to raise it.

The touchscreen

To cram all the information that you need onto one screen, HTC takes the modern approach to screen layout. You'll want to become familiar with several finger-navigation motions used to work with your screen.

Before diving in, though, here's a small list of terms you need to know:

✔ **Icon:** This is a little image. Tapping an icon launches an application or performs some function, such as making a telephone call.

✔ **Button:** A button on a touchscreen is meant to look like a three-dimensional button that you would push on, say, a telephone. Buttons are typically labeled to tell you what they do when you tap them. For example, you'll see buttons labeled Save or Send.

✔ **Hyperlink:** Sometimes called a *link* for short, a hyperlink is text that performs some function when you tap it. Usually text is lifeless. If you tap a word and it does nothing, then it's just text. If you tap a word and it launches a website or causes a screen to pop up, it's a hyperlink.

✔ **Thumbnail:** This is a small, low-resolution version of a larger, high-resolution picture stored somewhere else.

With this background, it's time discuss the motions you'll be using on the touchscreen.

You need to clean the touchscreen glass from time to time. The glass on your phone is Gorilla Glass (made by Corning) — the toughest stuff available to protect against breakage. Use a soft cloth or microfiber to get fingerprints off. You can even wipe the touchscreen on your clothes. However, never use a paper towel! Over time, glass is no match for the fibers in the humble paper towel.

Tap

Often you just tap the screen to make things happen (as when you launch an app) or select options. Think of a *tap* as like a single click of a mouse on a computer screen. A tap is simply a touch on the screen; much like using a touchscreen at a retail kiosk. Figure 2-10 shows what the tap motion should look like.

Figure 2-10: The tap motion.

One difference between a mouse click on a computer and a tap on an HTC One phone is that a single tap launches applications on the phone in the same way that a double-click of the mouse launches an application on a computer.

A tap is different from *press and hold* (see the next section). If you leave your finger on the screen for more than an instant, the phone thinks you want to do something other than launch an application.

Press and hold

Press and hold, as the name implies, involves putting your finger on an icon on the screen and leaving it there for more than a second. What happens when you leave your finger on an icon depends upon the situation.

For example, when you press and hold on an application on the Home screen (the screen that comes up after you turn on the phone), a garbage-can icon appears onscreen. This is to remove that icon from that screen. And when you press and hold an application icon from the list of applications, the phone assumes that you want to copy that application to your Home screen. Don't worry if these distinctions might not make sense yet. The point is that you should be familiar with holding and pressing — and that it's different from tapping.

You don't need to tap or press and hold very hard for the phone to know that you want it to do something. Neither must you worry about breaking the glass, even by pressing on it very hard. If you hold the phone in one hand and tap with the other, you'll be fine. I suppose you might break the glass on the phone if you put it on the floor and press up into a one-fingered handstand. I don't recommend that, but if you do try it, please post the video on YouTube.

On average, a person calls 911 about once every year. Usually, you call 911 because of a stressful situation. Like every phone, the HTC One has a special stress sensor that causes it to lock up when you need it most. Okay, not really, but it seems that way. When you're stressed, it's easy to think that you're tapping when you're actually pressing and holding. Be aware of this tendency and remember to *tap*.

Moving around the screen or to the next screen

Additional finger motions help you move around the screens and to adjust the scaling for images that you want on the screen. Mastering these motions is important to getting the most from your phone.

The first step is navigating the screen to access what's not visible onscreen. Think of this as navigating a regular computer screen, where you use a horizontal scroll bar to access information to the right or left of what's visible on your monitor, or a vertical scroll bar to move you up and down on a screen.

The same concept works on your phone. To overcome the practical realities of screen size on a phone that will fit into your pocket, the HTC One phone uses a *panorama* screen layout, meaning that you keep scrolling left or right (or maybe up and down) to access different screens.

In a nutshell, although the full width of a screen is accessible, only the part bounded by the physical screen of the HTC One phone is visible on the display. Depending upon the circumstances, you have several ways to get to information not visible on the active screen. These actions include drag, flicks, pinch and stretch, and double taps. I cover all these gestures in the following sections.

Drag

The simplest finger motion on the phone is the drag. You place your finger on a point on the screen and then drag the image with your finger. Then you lift your finger. Figure 2-11 shows what the motion looks like. Dragging allows you to move slowly around the panorama. This motion is like clicking a scroll bar and moving it slowly.

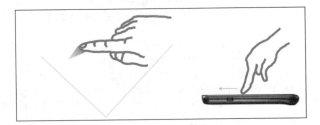

Figure 2-11: The drag motion for controlled movement.

Flick

To move quickly around the panorama, you can flick the screen to move in the direction of your flick (see Figure 2-12).

Better control of this motion comes with practice. In general, the faster the flick, the more the panorama moves. However, some screens (such as the extended Home screen) move only one screen to the right or left, no matter how fast you flick.

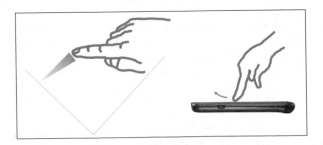

Figure 2-12: Use a flick motion for faster movement.

Pinch and stretch

Some screens allow you to change the scale of images you view on your screen. When this feature is active, the Zoom options change the magnification of the area on the screen. You can zoom out to see more features at a smaller size, or zoom in to see more detail at a larger size.

To zoom out, you put two fingers (apart) on the screen and pull them together to pinch the image. Make sure you're centered on the spot where you want to see in more detail. The pinch motion is shows in Figure 2-13.

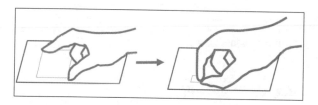

Figure 2-13: Use the pinch motion to zoom out.

The opposite motion zooms in. This involves the stretch motion, as shown in Figure 2-14. You place two fingers (close together) and stretch them apart.

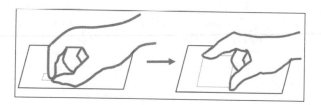

Figure 2-14: Use the stretch motion to zoom in.

Double tap

The double tap (shown in Figure 2-15) just means tapping the same button area on the screen twice in rapid succession. You use the double tap to jump between a zoomed-in and a zoomed-out image to get you back to the previous resolution. This option saves you frustration in getting back to a familiar perspective.

When you double-tap, time the taps so that the phone doesn't interpret them as two separate taps. With a little practice, you'll master the timing of the second tap.

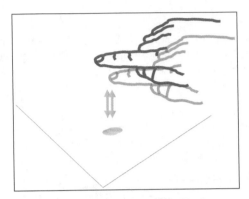

Figure 2-15: The double-tap motion.

The extended Home screen

If your HTC One is your first smartphone, let's take a moment and get you familiar with the idea of the Home screen. After all, the first screen you see on a feature phone is usually the dial-pad. You typically need to tap a button to get to the games and other non-calling options, such as your list of contacts.

Smartphones are different. You will use the HTC One phone as a phone as often as you did with your old phone, perhaps even more. However, you will probably find that you will call someone by dialing their number from a dial-pad less often than having your phone dial from your contact list, an email, from voice commands, or any of a bunch of new ways.

In recognition of this reality, you do not come to a dial-pad when you turn on your phone. You come to what is called the "Home screen." You can get to the telephone dial-pad from the home screen, but you can also get to your favorite tools on the phone from here.

In addition, you will find that a single page will not hold all your favorite icons, links, and gadgets (which I will define in a moment). The first screen that comes up is really a bunch of screens tied together to create the Extended Home screen. We call it Home screen, for short. HTC has set it to be four screen-widths wide and one screen high. You can practice your "drag" and "flick" motions on this page to navigate around.

The Home button

The biggest button on your phone is the Home button (see Figure 2-16). It's on the bottom of the front screen and looks like the outline of a house. (Clever. No?)

The Home button brings you back to the home screen from wherever you are in an application, game, or phone.

Home
Button

Figure 2-16: The HTC One Home button on the front.

If you're working on applications and feel like you're helplessly lost, don't worry. Press the Home button, close your eyes, tap your heels together three times, and think to yourself, "There's no place like home," and you will be brought back to the Home screen. (You don't really need to do all that other stuff after pressing the Home button. Just pressing the Home button does the trick.)

Four screens is the default setting. You can adjust this number, but there comes a point when so many screens become difficult to manage. Do yourself a favor and limit yourself to seven or eight.

The Extended Home screen is where you can organize icons and other functions to best make the phone convenient for you. Out of the box, HTC and your cellular carrier have worked together to create a starting point for you. Beyond that, though, you have lots of ways you can customize your Home screen for easy access to the things that are most important to you. Much of the book covers all the things that the phone can do, but a recurring theme is how to put your favorite capabilities on your Home screen if you wish.

To start, check out the layout of the Home screen and how it relates to other areas of the phone. Knowing these areas is important for basic navigation.

Other important buttons on the Home screen

Figure 2-17 shows a typical Home screen and highlights three important areas on the phone.

- ✔ **The notification area:** This part of the screen presents you with small icons that let you know if something important is up, like battery life.

- ✔ **The primary shortcuts:** These four or five icons remain stationary as you move across the home screen. HTC and your cellular carrier have determined that these are the five most important applications on your phone.

- ✔ **The Device Function keys:** These three keys control essential phone functions, regardless of what else is going on at the moment with the phone.

Adding shortcuts to the Home screen

As seen in Figure 2-17, you have a lot of screen real estate where you can put icons of your favorite applications. You can add shortcuts to the apps to the desired page on your Home panorama by following these steps:

1. From the desired Home screen, tap the Apps icon.

The apps icon (shown here) brings up all the apps you have installed on your phone.

2. Press and hold the apps you want to add.

Your screen will revert to your last Home page with an icon randomly placed on the screen. Now you just drag the app shortcut to where you want it. Done.

Figure 2-17: Important areas on the HTC One Home screen.

Taking away shortcuts

Say that you put the shortcut on the wrong screen. No problem. You can press and hold it, and then drag it left or right until it's on the screen you want. Taking a shortcut off your Home screen is simple too: Press and hold the shortcut on the screen. In a moment, a garbage can icon appears at the top of the screen. Drag the doomed shortcut to the garbage can, and off it goes to its maker.

It's gone, but if you made a mistake, you can get it back easily enough. To re-create it, simply go back to the App Menu key and follow the process again.

The notification area and screen

As shown in Figure 2-17, the notification area is at the top of the phone. You'll see little status icons there. Maybe you got a text or an email, or you'll notice that an application needs some tending to.

Think of the notification area as a special email inbox where your carrier (or even the phone itself) can give you important information about what's happening with your phone. The large icons at the top tell you the condition of the different radio systems on your phone: The number of bars shown gives you an indication of signal strength, and usually the phone will also tell you what kind of signal you're getting – such as 3G or 4G.

You could take the time to learn the meanings of all the little icons that might come up, but that would take you a while. A more convenient option is to touch the notification area and drag it down, as shown in Figure 2-18.

The rest of the screen is written so that you can understand what's going on — and what, if anything, you're expected to do. For example, if you see that you have a new email, you tap the text of the link, and you're taken to your new email.

When you're finished reading the notifications, you slide your finger back up to the top. If this screen gets too full, you can clear it by tapping the Clear button. You can also clear notifications one at a time by touching each one and swiping it to the side.

The primary shortcuts

The *primary shortcuts* are what HTC and your cellular carrier decided on as the four or five most important functions of your phone. Each phone type has its own twist on this idea, but these icons remain the same across all the Home pages.

Among the other possible shortcuts here are shortcuts that take you to your contacts, your email, the Internet, texting/messaging, or your list of applications. The good news is that you can change any of these to icons you prefer. To delete a primary shortcut, press and hold. The garbage can icon will appear at the top. Just drag the icon into the trash. To put in a different icon, just drag the desired app to this area of the home page.

Figure 2-18: Notification pull-down screen.

The Device Function keys

At the bottom of the screen, below the rectangular screen display, are three important buttons, the Device Function keys. Whatever else you're doing on the phone, these buttons can take over. We have already discussed the Home button.

The Device Function keys are kind of cool because they light up when you're touching them or the screen, and fade away the rest of the time.

The Recent Apps button

The button to the right of the Home button is called the Recent Apps button. Tapping the button once brings up a list of the apps that are open. This is a slick way to navigate between running apps. You can also shut all the apps down by tapping the "x." This will help you save some battery life.

The key to the left of the Home button is a Return key. If it's lit, you can tap it and it will take you back one step.

The Back button

The Back button on your phone is similar to the Back button in a web browser: It takes you back one screen.

As you start navigating through the screens on your phone, tapping the Back button takes you back to the previous screen. If you keep tapping the Back button, you'll eventually return to the Home screen.

The keyboard

The screen of the HTC One phone is important, but you'll still probably spend more time on the keyboard entering data on the QWERTY keyboard.

Using the software keyboard

The software keyboard automatically pops up when the application detects a need for user text input. The keyboard appears at the bottom of the screen.

For example, say you're in Seattle, searching for the Seattle Art Museum via the Mapping application. Tap the Search button, and the keyboard pops up onscreen.

In this case, a text box pops up in addition to the keyboard. As you type Seattle Art Museum, the text appears in the box on the screen as if you had typed it on a hardware keyboard. The phone is smart enough to know when the keyboard should appear and disappear. If the keyboard doesn't appear when you want to start typing, you can tap on the text box where you want to enter data.

Using Voice Recognition

The third option for a keyboard is . . . no keyboard at all! HTC One phones come with voice recognition as an option. It's very easy, and works surprisingly well. In most spots where you have an option to enter text, you see a small version of a microphone.

Just tap this icon and say what you would have typed. You see the phone thinking for a second, and then it shows a screen that looks like Figure 2-19.

Figure 2-19: The Voice Recognition screen.

When you're done, you can tap the Done button, or just be quiet and wait. Within a few seconds, you'll see what you said!

The orientation of the phone

In the earlier section where I discuss the Power button, I refer to the phone being in vertical orientation (so that the phone is tall and narrow). It can also be used in the *landscape* orientation (sideways, or so that the phone is short and wide). The phone senses in which direction you're holding it, and orients the screen to make it easier for you to view.

Not all applications can change their display. That nuance is left to the writers of the application. For example, your phone can play videos. However, the video player application that comes with your phone shows video in landscape mode only.

In addition, the phone can sense when you're holding it to your ear. When it senses that it's held in this position, it shuts off the screen. You need not be concerned that you'll accidentally "chin-dial" a number in Botswana.

Going to Sleep Mode/Turning Off the Phone

You can leave your phone on every minute until you're ready to upgrade to the newest HTC One phone in a few years, but that would use up your battery in no time. Instead, put your idle phone in sleep mode to save battery power. ***Note:*** Your phone goes into sleep mode automatically after 30 seconds of inactivity on the screen.

You can adjust the sleep time out for a longer duration, which I cover in Chapter 16. Or you can manually put the phone in sleep mode by pressing the Power button for just a moment.

Sometimes it's best to simply shut down the phone if you aren't going to use it for several days or more or the flight attendant tells you it's required. To shut down the phone completely, simply press and hold the Power button for a few seconds. The following options appear:

- **Silent mode:** Turn off sound, but vibrate if there is an important notification like an incoming call or text.

- **Airplane mode:** Turns off the radios that communicate to the local Wi-Fi access point and the cellular network so that you can't receive or make voice calls or send or receive texts or data. As the name implies, use this setting when you're flying. If you want to use applications that can operate without a data connection, such as some games, you can. The good news: Because some flights now provide Wi-Fi, the phone *does* allow you to turn Wi-Fi back on when you're in airplane mode if you need it.

- **Power Off:** Shut down the phone completely.

Good night!

Part II
Communications

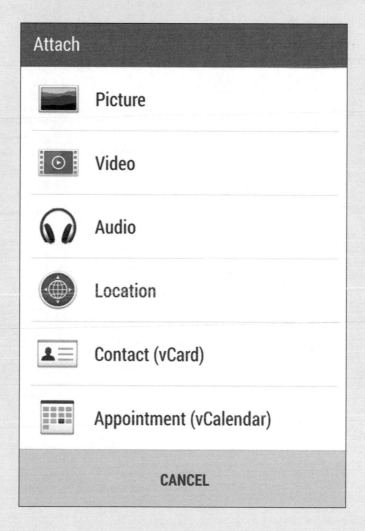

In this part . . .

- Dial and answer phone calls.
- Connect to a Bluetooth headset.
- Send and receive text messages.
- Set up email accounts on your phone.
- Get all your contacts in one location.

riah Heap
H: (425) 555-1212

LAST CALL
Medina, WA

Uriah Heap
↙ H: (425) 555-1

CALL
WA

Uriah Heap
↙ H: (425) 555-1212

LAST CALL
Medina, WA

3

Calling People

. . . .

In This Chapter

▶ Dialing and answering phone calls

▶ Using your call list

▶ Making emergency calls

▶ Connecting to a Bluetooth headset

. . . .

*A*t its essence, any cellphone — no matter how fancy or smart — exists to make phone calls. The good news is that making and receiving phone calls on your HTC One is easy.

In this chapter, I show you not only how to make a call but also how to use your call list to keep track of your calls. And don't skip the section on using your phone for emergencies.

Finally, if you're like many people, you're never doing just one thing at a time, and a Bluetooth headset can make it easier for you to talk on the phone while driving and getting directions, checking email, wrangling kids and dogs, or just plain living life. In this chapter, I show you how to hook up your phone to a Bluetooth headset so you can make and receive phone calls hands-free.

Making Calls

After your phone is on and you're connected to your cellular carrier (see Chapters 1 and 2), you can make a phone call. It all starts from the Home screen. Along the bottom of the screen, above the Device Function keys, are five icons, which are the *primary shortcuts* (see Figure 3-1). From left to right, they are

- ✔ Phone
- ✔ Messaging
- ✔ Apps menu
- ✔ Internet
- ✔ Camera

Figure 3-1: The primary shortcuts on the Home screen.

To make a call, follow these steps:

1. **From the Home screen, tap the phone icon.**

   The keypad screen (see Figure 3-2) appears. This looks like a stylized version of a touch pad on a regular landline phone.

Without Telephone Number   With Telephone Number

Figure 3-2: Dial the number from the keypad screen.

2. **Tap the telephone number you want to call.**

   Don't be alarmed if you don't hear a dial tone until you tap Send; smart-phones don't connect to a network and start a dial tone until after you dial your number.

   For long-distance calls while in the United States, you don't need to dial 1 before the area code — just dial the area code and then the seven-digit phone number. Similarly, you can include the "1 and the area code for local calls. On the other hand, if you're traveling internationally, you need to include the 1 — and be prepared for international roaming charges!

   In Chapter 6, you can read about how to make a phone call through your contacts.

3. **Tap the green Call button (towards the bottom of the screen) to place the call.**

   Within a few seconds, you should hear the phone ringing or giving a busy signal.

4. **When you're done, tap the End Call button (the red button at the bottom of the screen).**

   The call is disconnected.

If the call doesn't go through, either the cellular coverage where you are is insufficient, or your phone got switched to Airplane mode. (It's possible, of course, that your cellular carrier let you out the door without having set you up for service, but that's pretty unlikely!)

Check the notification section at the top of the screen. If there are no connection-strength bars, try moving to another location. If you see a small airplane silhouette, bring down the notification screen (see how in Chapter 2) and tap the plane icon to turn off Airplane mode.

Answering Calls

Receiving a call is even easier than making a call. When someone calls you, caller ID information appears along with three icons. Figure 3-3 shows a typical screen for an incoming call. To answer the call, tap the green Answer button.

In Part IV, I fill you in on some exciting options that you can enable (or not) when you get a call. For example, you can specify a unique ringtone for a particular number, or have an image of the caller pop up (if you store contacts to your phone).

Regardless of what you were doing on the phone at that moment — such as listening to music or playing a game — the answer screen can appear. Any active application, including music or video, is suspended until the call is over.

Figure 3-3: You're getting a call.

For callers to leave you messages, you must set up your voicemail. If you haven't yet set up your voicemail, the caller will hear a recorded message saying that your voicemail account isn't yet set up. Some cellular carriers can set up voicemail for you when you activate the account and get the phone; others require you to set up voicemail on your own. Ask how voicemail works at your carrier store or look for instructions in the manual included with your phone.

HTC One for lazybones: Automatic answering

Imagine this scenario: You show up to work, and two co-workers have called in sick. You spend your day hustling to cover for them. You get home and clean the house. It has snowed, so you need to shovel your (as well as for the elderly widow's next door's) walk and driveway. (You are just that kind of person.)

All you want to do is flop down on the sofa, but then your HTC One rings. It is your best friend.

By then pure exhaustion has kicked in, and you just don't have it in you to tap that green Answer button.

No need to worry! Your HTC One has you taken care of. Simply put the phone to your ear! After a moment, the phone answers for you. Using this feature requires a special level of laziness, which is why I am so fond of it!

Not Taking Calls Today

The Decline and Answer buttons are pretty standard on any cellular phone. However, your HTC One is no standard phone. You have a number of options if you want to decline to answer a call.

The first option to not answer a call is to simply ignore the ringing. If the ringing bothers you, you can tap the red Decline button. The ringing stops immediately. In either case, the call goes to voicemail. You can handle the call you do not want to or can't answer other ways:

- Putting the phone face down. This mutes the phone and the caller goes to voicemail.
- Decline the call and give yourself a reminder to call the person back.
- Decline and immediately send a text to the caller.

You get to make your choice on using the reminder or the text when you tap the button that says Decline. When you tap Decline, you get the pop-up screen in Figure 3-4.

If you choose to remind yourself, a notification will appear with the caller ID information. If you choose a text, some of the typical "canned" messages that you can send are

- I'm in class.
- Call you later.
- Can't talk. Text me.

✔ Can't talk now. I will call you soon.

✔ I'm in a meeting.

Decline call

You declined the call. By pressing these buttons, you can:

Remind me

Send text

Don't show this again ☐

CANCEL

Figure 3-4: Decline a call if you want.

You tap the message that applies (but not while you're driving). The message is sent as a text right away, which alerts the caller that you're not ignoring him or her — it's just that you can't talk right now. Nice touch.

You can also create and store your own message, like "Go away and leave me alone," or "Whatever I am doing is more important than talking to you." You could also be polite. To create your own canned message, tap the blank text box and type away. It's stored on your phone for when you need it.

The caller has to be able to receive text messages on the phone used to make the call. This feature doesn't work if your caller is calling from a landline or a cellphone that can't receive texts.

Keeping Track of Your Calls: The Call List

Sure, you might have caller ID on your landline at home or work, but most landline phones don't keep track of who you called. Cellphones, on the other hand, can keep track of all the numbers you called. This information can be very convenient, like when you want to return a call, and you don't have that number handy. In addition, you can easily add a number to the contact list on your phone. (More about that in Chapter 6.)

Once you've made your first call, you will see that the phone dialing pad includes your last call. Figure 3-5 shows an example.

Figure 3-5: The dial screen with the last call.

Your phone assumes that the last call you made has the best chance of being your next call. This is bound to be the case some of the time. If not, you can simply tap the call history icon (just underneath the word Phonebook).

Sliding this link to the right will bring up the screen seen in Figure 3-6, which includes the information on your most recent calls.

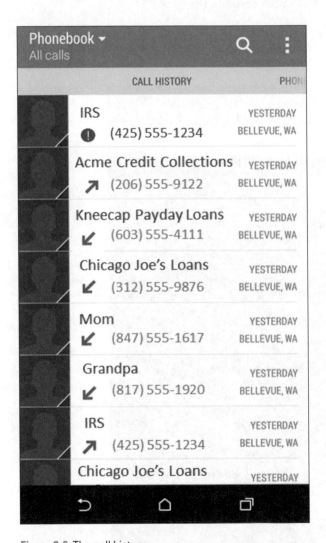

Figure 3-6: The call history.

Each call bears an icon telling you whether it was an

- **Outgoing call you made:** An arrow points down and to the left towards the image.
- **Incoming call you received:** An arrow points up and to the right.

> ✔ **Incoming call you ignored or missed:** A red exclamation mark with the calling number in red.

Tapping any number in your call list automatically calls that number.

Making an Emergency Call: The 411 on 911

Cellphones are wonderful tools for calling help in an emergency. The HTC One, like all phones in the United States and Canada, can make emergency calls to 911.

Just tap the phone icon on the Home screen, tap 911, and then tap Send.

You'll be routed to the 911 call center nearest to your location. This works wherever you're at within the United States. So, say you live in Chicago but have a car accident in Charlotte; just tap 911 to be connected to the 911 call center in Charlotte, not Chicago.

No problem, even if your phone isn't registered on a network (as your battery is charged). Your phone lets you know that the only number you can dial is a 911 call center, even if the Home screen is locked.

When you call 911 from a landline, the address you're calling from is usually displayed for the operator. When you're calling from a cellphone, though, the operator doesn't have that specific information. Take a moment and come up with a good description of where you are — the street you're on, the nearest cross street (if you know it), any businesses or other landmarks nearby.

So, when you call 911, the operator might say, "911. *Where* is your emergency?" Don't let this question throw you; after all, you're probably focused on *what* is happening and not on *where*. An operator who knows where you are is in a better position to help you with your emergency. Your phone does have a GPS receiver in it that 911 centers can access. However, it's not always accurate; it may not be receiving location information at that moment, as is the case when you're indoors.

When you're outside the United States or Canada, 911 might not be the number you call in an emergency. Mexico uses 066, 060, or 080, but most tourist areas also accept 911. And most— but not all— of Europe uses 112. Knowing the local emergency number is as important as knowing enough of the language to say you need help.

Whoops — you accidentally dialed 911

If you accidentally dial 911 from your phone, don't hang up. Just tell the operator that it was an accidental call. She might ask some questions to verify that you are indeed safe and not being forced to say that your call was an accident.

If you panic and hang up after accidentally dialing 911, you'll get a call from the nearest 911 call center. Always answer the call, even if you feel foolish. If you don't answer the call, the 911 call centers will assume that you're in trouble and can't respond. They'll track you down from the GPS in your phone to verify that you're safe. If you thought you'd feel foolish explaining your mistake to a 911 operator, imagine how foolish you'd feel explaining it to the police officer who tracks you down and is upset with you for wasting the department's time.

Synching a Bluetooth Headset

With a Bluetooth headset device, you can talk on your phone without holding it to your ear and without any cords running from the phone to your earpiece. You've probably come across plenty of people talking on Bluetooth headsets. You might even have wondered whether they were a little crazy, talking to themselves. Well, call yourself crazy now, because when you start using a Bluetooth headset, you might never want to go back.

Be aware of *bluejacking* (tricks that thieves use to get access to your phone via Bluetooth). Chapter 17 tells you what they are.

The first step to using a Bluetooth headset with your HTC One is to *sync* (coordinate) the two devices. Here's how:

1. **From the Home screen on your phone, tap the apps icon.**

   This gets you to the list of all the applications on your phone.

2. **Flick or pan to the settings icon and tap it.**

   The settings icon is shown to the left. This screen holds most of the settings that you can adjust on your phone. If you prefer, you can also bring down the notification screen and tap the gear icon or tap the menu button on the Home screen. All these actions will get you to the same place.

   Tapping the Settings icon brings up the screen in Figure 3-7.

3. **Tap the Bluetooth line.**

   This brings up Figure 3-8.

   Be sure that the green button to the right is set to On. If the button happens to be in the Off position, go ahead and tap it so that it toggles to the On position.

When you open this screen, your phone will automatically start looking for other Bluetooth devices. This will last for 120 seconds — enough time for you to get your Bluetooth device into pairing mode. That way both devices can negotiate the proper security settings and pair up every time they "see" each other from now on. See Figure 3-7 to see that it is in scanning mode. (If you can't get your Bluetooth devices ready in time, you can close and re-open this screen, or you can tap the bar at the bottom with the words Scan.)

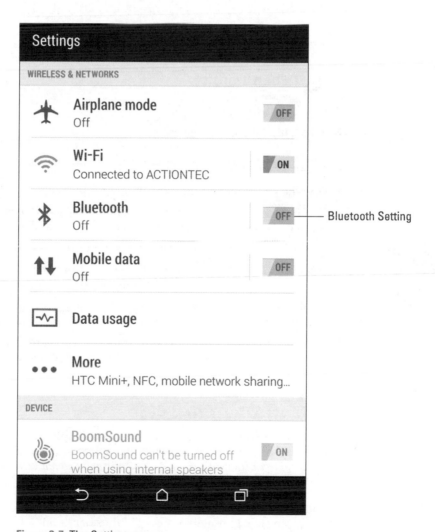

Figure 3-7: The Settings screen.

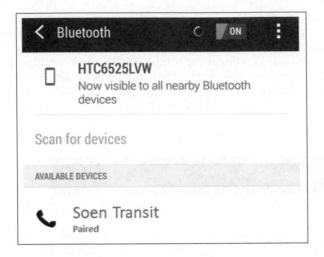

Figure 3-8: The Bluetooth settings screen.

4. **Put your headset into sync mode.**

   Follow the instructions that came with your headset.

   After a moment, the phone "sees" the headset. When it does, you're prompted to enter the security code, and the software keyboard pops up.

5. **Enter the security code for your headset and then tap the Enter button.**

   The security code on most headsets is 0000, but check the instructions that came with your headset if that number doesn't work.

   Your phone might see other devices in the immediate area. If so, it asks which device you want to pair with. Tap the name of your headset.

   Your headset is now synced to your phone. If you turn one on when the other is already on, they recognize each other and automatically pair up.

Options Other than Headsets

Headsets aren't the only option. Although many people walk around with the ubiquitous Bluetooth headset dangling from an ear, you have other choices: Sync to all kinds of Bluetooth devices, including external keyboards, laptops, tablets, external speakers, and even your car.

You can buy external sensors for measuring blood pressure, heart rate, and a lot of other physical information. Some of these are built into wearable devices, like a fitness bracelet. Manufacturers are now embedding computers into home appliances that can connect to your smartphone through Bluetooth!

The good news is that regardless of the technology, you can connect all these devices to your phone simply by using the steps described here.

4

Discovering the Joy of Text

In This Chapter

▶ Sending a text message
▶ Sending a text message with an attachment
▶ Receiving a text message

*S*ure, cellphones are made for talking. But these days, many people use their cellphones even more for texting. *Text messages* (short messages, usually 160 characters or less, sent by cellphone) are particularly convenient when you can't talk at the moment (maybe you're in a meeting or class) or when you just have a small bit of information to share ("Running late — see you soon!").

Many cellphone users — particularly younger ones — prefer sending texts to making a phone call, saying that texting is faster and more convenient. They often use texting shorthand (such as "r u" instead of "are you") to fit more content in that character limit.

Even the most basic phones support texting these days, but your HTC One makes sending and receiving text messages more convenient, no matter whether you're an occasional or pathological texter. In this chapter, I fill you in on how to send a text message (with or without an attachment), how to receive a text message, and how to read your old text messages.

 Location

 Contact (vCard)

 Appointment (vCalendar)

CANCEL

To use text messaging, you must have texting capability as part of your service plan. See Chapter 1 for more info.

This chapter uses images from the Android Messaging application. It is possible that your phone may have as its default the Verizon Message app or another texting application. If so, you can easily switch to the Messaging app. You can also use the default app, but the images will be somewhat different. Your choice.

Sending the First Text Message

There are two scenarios for texting. The first is when you send someone a text for the first time. The second is when you have a text conversation with a person.

When you first get your phone and are ready to brag about your new HTC One phone and want to send a text to your best friend, here's how easy it is:

1. **On the Home screen, tap the messaging icon.**

   The Messaging application is between the contacts and the Internet icons. When you tap it, you get a mostly blank Home screen for texting. When you have some conversations going, it begins to fill up. More on that soon.

2. **Tap the new message icon (the plus sign hovering over a blank page).**

   Tapping the new message icon brings up the screen in Figure 4-1.

3. **Tap to enter the recipient's ten-digit mobile telephone number.**

   A text box appears at the top of the screen with the familiar To field at the top. The keyboard appears at the bottom of the screen. As shown in Figure 4-2, the top field is where you type in the telephone number. The numerals are along the top of the keyboard.

   Be sure to include the area code, even if the person you're texting is local. There's no need to include 1 before the number.

   If this is your first text, you haven't had a chance to build up a history of texts. After you've been using your messaging application for a while, your phone will start trying to anticipate your intended recipient.

Figure 4-1: A blank texting screen.

4. **To type your text message, tap the text box that says Enter Message. Figure 4-3 shows you where to enter your text.**

   Your text message can be up to 160 characters, including spaces and punctuation. The application counts down the number of characters you have left, as you can see in Figure 4-3 above the messaging icon.

Figure 4-2: Type the recipient's number in the upper text box.

Your texting app will probably try to autocorrect a misspelled word. You may find it handy or you may find it annoying. If you want evidence as to why checking its handiwork is a good idea, search online for **funny autocorrect examples** (although some are racy).

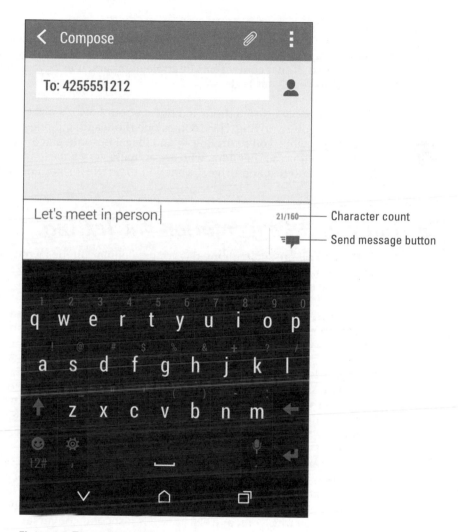

Figure 4-3: Type your text here.

5. **Send the text by tapping the send message icon.**

   The Send Message button is orange. The phone takes it from here. Within a few seconds, the message is sent to your friend's cellphone.

After you build your contact list (read about this in Chapter 6), you can tap a name from the contact list or start typing a name in the recipient text box. If there's only one number for that contact, your phone assumes that's who you want to text. If that contact has multiple numbers, it asks you which phone number to send your text to.

You've probably heard a thousand times about how it's a very bad idea to text while you're driving. Here comes one-thousand-and-one. It's a *very bad idea* to text while you're driving — and illegal in some places. There are Dummies who read this book who are actually very smart, and then there are DUMMIES who text and drive. I want you to be the former and not the latter.

Carrying on a Conversation via Texting

In the bad ol' pre-smartphone days, most cellular phones would keep a log of your texts. The phone kept the texts that you sent or received in sequential order, regardless of who sent or received them.

Texts stored sequentially are old school. Your HTC One tracks the contact with whom you've been texting and stores each set of back-and-forth messages as a *conversation*.

In Figure 4-4, you can see that the first page for messaging holds *conversations*. After you start texting someone, those texts are stored in one conversation. As Figure 4-4 shows, each text message is presented in sequence, with the author of the text indicated by the alignment of the text on the page and whether the text is in a box (their message) or not (your message).

Note the Add Text box at the bottom of the screen. With this convenient feature, you can send whatever you type to the person with whom you're having a conversation. In the bad old days, it was sometimes hard to keep straight the different texting conversations you were having. When you start a texting conversation with someone else, there is a second conversation.

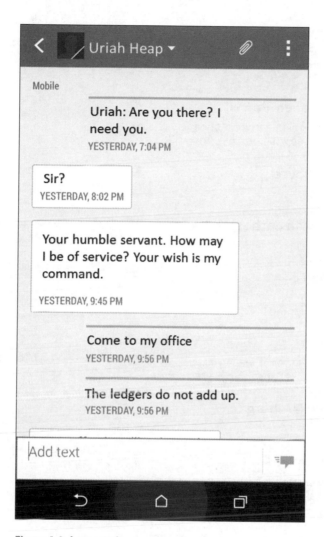

Figure 4-4: A messaging conversation.

Before too long, you'll have multiple conversations going on. Don't worry. They aren't the kind of conversations you need to keep going constantly. No one thinks twice if you don't text for a while. The image in Figure 4-5 shows how the text page from Figure 4-1 can look before too long.

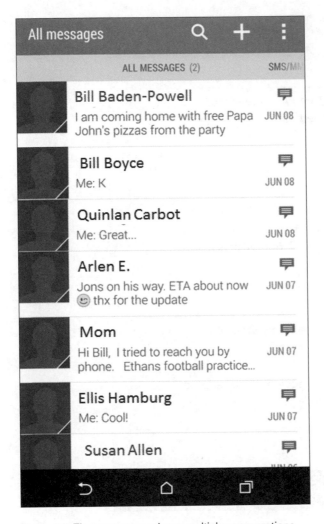

Figure 4-5: The text screen shows multiple conversations.

Sending an Attachment with a Text

What if you want to send a picture, some music, or a Word document along with your text? Easy as pie, as long as the phone on the receiving end can recognize the attachment. Here is the recipe:

1. **From the Home screen, tap the messaging icon.**

2. **Either tap the plus sign, enter the number of the intended recipient, or pick up on an existing conversation.**

You'll see the text creation page from Figure 4-2. Enter the information you want like a normal text.

3. **To add an attachment, tap the icon that looks like a paper clip.**

   The paper-clip icon brings up the screen you see in Figure 4-6.

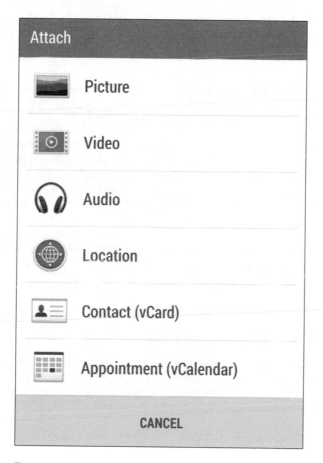

Figure 4-6: You can attach different kinds of files to a text.

4. **Tap your choice of file type.**

   This screen asks what kind of file you want to attach. Your choices include pictures, videos, audio files, and some others I describe later. For now, it's just good that you know you have options.

   After you select the file, it becomes an attachment to your text message.

5. **Continue typing your text message, if needed.**

6. **When you're done with the text portion of the message, tap the Send Text button, and off it all goes.**

A simple text message is an SMS (short message service) message. When you add an attachment, you're sending an MMS (multimedia messaging service) message. Back in the day, MMS messages cost more to send and receive than SMS messages did. These days, that isn't the case in the United States.

Receiving Text Messages

Receiving a text is even easier than sending one.

When you're having a text conversation and you get a new text from the person you're texting with, your phone beeps or vibrates. Also, the screen's notification area (the very top) shows a very small version of the messaging icon. You can either pull down the notification screen from the very top of the screen or start the messaging application. Your choice. If an attachment comes along, it's included in the conversation screens.

To access the text, you need to unlock the screen. The messaging icon (an envelope) also displays the number of new texts that you have. Tap that icon to open the conversations.

Managing Your Text History

The Messaging Conversations screen stores and organizes all your texts until you delete them. You should clean up this screen every now and then. I recommend being vicious in deleting the older texts and conversations. Trust me; deleting all your old messages can be cathartic!

The simplest option for managing your messages is to

1. **Tap the menu icon (three vertical dots).**

2. **Tap Delete Threads.**

3. **Select all the conversations that you want deleted.**

4. **Tap the Delete link at the bottom of the screen, and they disappear.**

Another deletion option is to open the conversation. You can delete each text by pressing and holding the balloon. After a moment, a menu appears from which you can delete that message. This method is a lot slower if you have lots of texts, though.

Sending and Receiving Email

In This Chapter

▶ Setting up email accounts on your phone
▶ Reading email on your phone
▶ Managing your email folder
▶ Sending email from your phone

I f you've had email on your phone for a while, you know how convenient it is. If the HTC One is the first cellphone you've had that can send and receive email, prepare to be hooked.

I start this chapter by showing you how to set up your email, regardless of whether your email program is supported (more on that in a bit). Then I show you how to read and manage your emails. Finally, I tell you how to write and send emails.

Using email on your phone requires a data connection. Some cellular carriers solve this problem by obliging you to have a data plan with your phone. If your cellular carrier does not, you won't be able to use email unless you're connected to a Wi-Fi hotspot. I strongly recommend that you get that data plan and enjoy the benefits of wireless email.

~~unt@example.com~~

Password

☐ Show password

☐ Send email from this account default

Setting Up Your Email

These days, many of us have multiple personal email address for many reasons. Your phone's Email app can manage up to ten email accounts. With an HTC One (unlike some other phones), you may need to create a separate email account just for your phone. If you go that route, however, you'll miss out on so many exciting capabilities. You need a Gmail account to access the Google Play Store that you use to download new applications for your phone. A Gmail account is also the means you use to back up your contacts and calendar — and it offers access to sharing photos. Without a Gmail account, you miss out on many of the best features on the HTC One.

Your phone mainly interacts with your inbox on your email account. It isn't really set up to work like the full-featured email application on your computer, though. For example, many email packages integrate with a sophisticated word processor, have sophisticated filing systems for your saved messages, and offer lots of fonts. As long as you don't mind working without these advanced capabilities, you might never need to get on your computer to access your email again, and you could store emails in folders on your phone. In practice, however, phone access to email is best used in working with emails that are in your inbox.

I highly recommend setting up a new Gmail account if you don't have one already (more on that later). Also, because setup is so easy, and makes you so productive, consider adding *all* your email accounts to your phone.

The Email app on your phone routinely polls all the email systems for which you identify an email account and password. It then presents you with copies of your emails.

Getting ready

In general, connecting to a personal email account simply involves entering the name of your email account and its password in your phone. Have these handy when you're ready to set up your phone.

You do need to pick one account as your favorite. Although you can send an email using any of the accounts, your phone wants to know the email account that you want it to use as a default.

Next, you may want to have access to your work account. This is relatively common these days, but some companies see this as a security problem. You should consult with your IT department for some extra information. Technologically, it's not hard to make this kind of thing happen as long as your business email is reasonably modern.

The advantages of getting a Gmail account

You might already have work and personal email accounts. You might even have an old email account that you check only once in a while because some friends, for whatever reason, haven't updated their profile for you and continue to use an old address.

The thought of getting yet another email address, even one that's free, might (understandably) be unappealing. After all, it's another address and password to remember. However, some important functions on your phone require a Gmail account:

✔ The ability to buy applications from the Play Store. (This is huge!) I go over the Play Store in Chapter 8.

✔ Free access to the photo site Picasa (although other sites have many of the same features). I cover Picasa and photo options in Chapter 9.

✔ Access to the Music and Video Hub. These slick services are explained in Chapter 12.

✔ Automatic backup of your contacts and calendar. That's explained in more detail in Chapters 6 and 13.

To make a long story short, it's worth the trouble to get a Gmail account, even if you already have a personal email account.

Setting up your existing Gmail account

If you already have a Gmail account, setting it up on your phone is easy as can be. Follow these steps from the Apps menu:

1. **Find the Gmail icon in the Apps list.**

   Here is the most confusing part. The icon on the left in Figure 5-1 is the Gmail app. The icon on the right is for all your other email accounts.

Figure 5-1: The mail icons in the Apps list.

2. **Tap the Gmail icon.**

   Because your phone doesn't know if you have a Gmail account, it asks you whether this is a new account.

3. **Tap the Existing button on the screen.**

   This brings up the screen in Figure 5-2.

Figure 5-2: The Gmail sign-in screen.

4. **Enter your existing Gmail user ID and password.**

5. **When you're ready, tap Done on the keyboard.**

   You may get a pop-up re-confirming that you agree with the terms of use and all that legal stuff. Tap OK. You'll see lots of flashing lights and whirling circles while your phone and your Gmail account get to know each other.

   If everything is correct, your phone and your account get acquainted and become best friends. After a few minutes, they are ready to serve your needs. If you have a problem, you probably mistyped something. Try retyping your information.

From this point on, any email you get on your Gmail account will also appear on your phone!

Setting up a new Gmail account

If you need to set up a new Gmail account, you have a few more steps to follow. Before you get into the steps, think up a good user ID and password.

Gmail has been around for a while. That means all the good, simple email addresses are taken. Unless you plan to start using this email account as your main email, which you could do if you wanted, you're probably best off if you pick some unusual combination of letters and numbers that you can remember for now to get through this process.

Follow these steps:

1. **Find the Gmail icon in the Apps list.**

2. **Tap the Gmail icon.**

3. **Tap the New button.**

4. **Enter your first and last names on the screen, and tap Next.**

   Google asks for your name. This is how they personalize any communications they have with you.

5. **Enter the username you want to use with Gmail and tap Done.**

   Hopefully you get this name approved on the first shot. If your first choice isn't available, try again. There is no easy way to check before you go these steps. Eventually, you hit on an unused ID. When you're successful, it will congratulate you.

6. **Accept the terms and conditions of the account.**

   You may want a lawyer to review this. Or not. Basically, the terms are that you should be nice and not try to cheat anyone. Don't abuse the privilege of having the account.

7. **Verify the funny-looking writing.**

   Google wants to make sure that you're a real person and not a computer program out to clog up a valid user ID. You will see a screen that looks like Figure 5-3.

Figure 5-3: The Authenticating screen.

8. **Prepare a security question and an alternate email address.**

   If you forget your password, Google wants to verify that you're really you and not someone pretending to be you. Google does this by asking you a security question and then asking for another email account where they can send your temporary password. These screens in Figure 5-4 show you where to enter your information and the question choices.

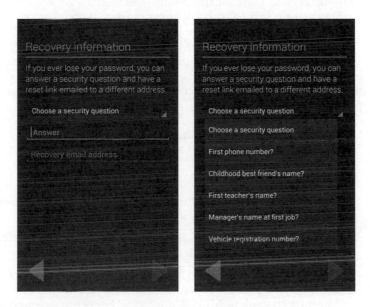

Figure 5-4: The Recovery Information screens.

9. **Join Google+ if you want.**

   The next screen asks if you want to join Google+. You can if you want, but I suggest that you come back to that question another time. The sooner you get your Gmail account set up, the more fun you can have.

10. **Tap Done.**

    Light flashes and you see a screen that says the cellphone is checking server settings. It usually takes much less than five minutes. While you wait, you'll see all kinds of messages that it's getting ready to sync things. Don't worry. I'll explain these messages in good time. For now, you can add any other email accounts you want by following the steps in the next section.

Working with non-Gmail email accounts

Your phone is set up to work with up to ten email accounts. If you have more than ten accounts, I'm thinking that you might have too much going on in your life. No phone, not even the HTC One, can help you there!

To set up an email account other than Gmail to work with your phone, go to the Home screen. Look for the simple mail icon; it has an envelope icon on it (see Figure 5-1). This is probably on your Home screen as one of the primary shortcuts just above the Device Function keys or in your application list.

After you tell your phone all your emails, the first Email screen will have all your emails from all your email accounts. This allows you to look at all the messages. In addition, each account has its own inbox. You can choose which option works best for you.

1. **Tap the menu icon from the Email screen.**

   This brings up a menu that looks like Figure 5-5.

2. **Tap Other.**

   This is a generic way to enter lots of kinds of email accounts. Tapping it brings up a screen that looks like Figure 5-6.

3. **Carefully enter your full email account name, and then enter your password in the second field.**

   Your email address should include the full shebang, including the @ sign and everything that follows it. Enter your password correctly, being careful with capitalization if your email server is case sensitive (most are). If in doubt, select the option that lets you see your password.

4. **Decide whether you want this account to be your default email account.**

   After you add multiple accounts to your phone, only one account can be your primary, or default, account. Although you can send an email from any of the accounts registered on your phone, you have to select one as the default. If you want this account to be the main account, select the Send Email from This Account by Default check box. If not, leave that option as it is.

5. **Tap Next.**

   You see all kinds of options you can select. Just go with the default settings for now.

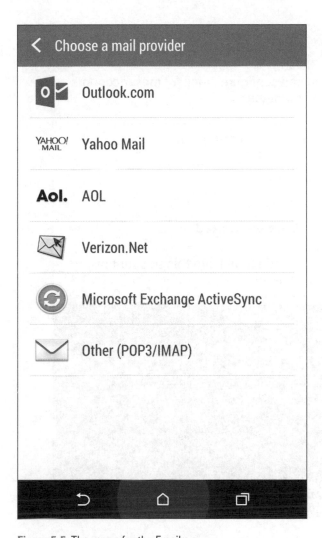

Figure 5-5: The menu for the Email app.

6. **Tap OK.**

   If everything goes as planned, your phone and your email account will start chatting.

7. **Enter names for the new email account.**

   You can always use the email address for the name, but I recommend choosing something shorter, like Joe's MSN or My Hotmail.

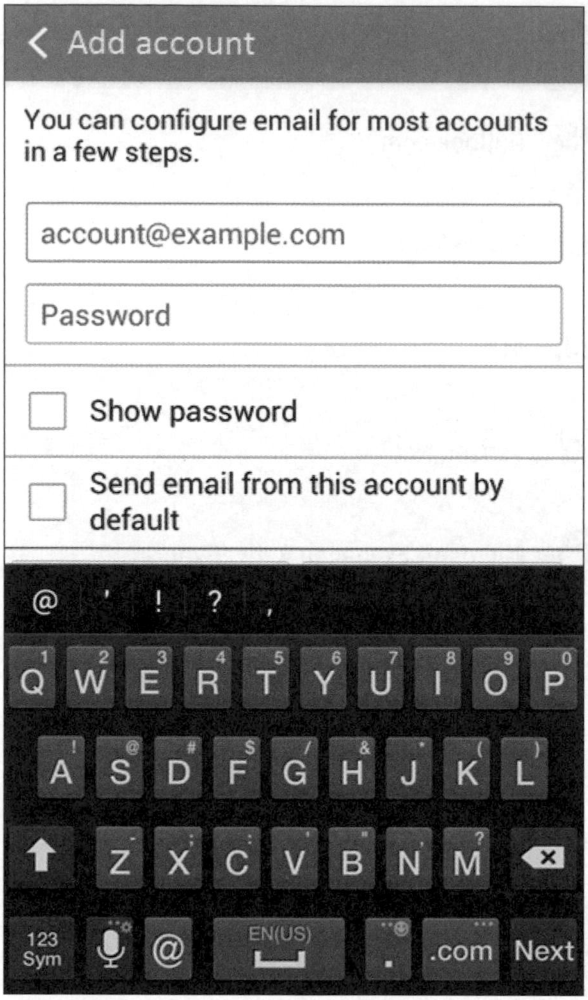

Figure 5-6: The Add Account screen.

8. **Tap Done.**

   Using Figure 5-7 as an example, you can see that my account is now registered on my phone. It worked!

Check that everything has gone as planned and is set up to your liking. Go back to the Home screen, tap the email icon, open Settings, and tap Add Account.

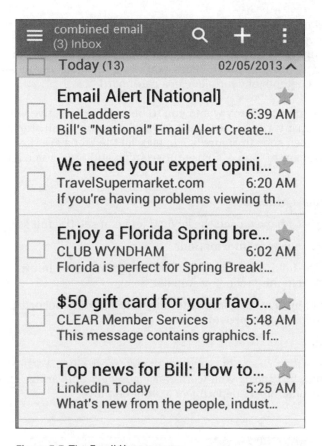

Figure 5-7: The Email Home screen.

Setting up a corporate email account

In addition to personal email accounts, you can add your work email to your phone — if it's based upon a Microsoft Exchange server, that is, and if it's okay with your company's IT department.

Before you get started, you need some information from the IT department of your company:

✔ The domain name of the office email server

✔ Your work email password

✔ The name of your exchange server

If the folks in IT are okay with you using your phone to access its email service, your IT department will have no trouble supplying you with this information.

Before you set up your work email on your phone, make sure that you have permission. If you do this without the green light from your company, and you end up violating your company's rules, you could be in hot water. Increasing your productivity won't be much help if you're standing out in the parking lot holding all the contents of your office in a cardboard box.

Assuming that your company wants you to be more productive with no extra cost to the company, the process for adding your work email starts at your email Home screen seen in Figure 5-5. In fact, all the steps are the same as the previous section up to Step 4, so use those steps and then come back here in place of Step 5.

1. **Tap Manual Setup.**

   In Figure 5-8, I have closed the keypad and can see the full screen.

2. **Enter your account information.**

   Some of the fields might be populated based upon the information that you entered in the preceding step list.

3. **Verify that information and enter any missing data according to what your IT department provided you.**

4. **Tap Next.**

   This begins the process of syncing with your work email. Within a minute, you should start seeing your work email messages appearing. If this doesn't happen, contact the IT department at your employer.

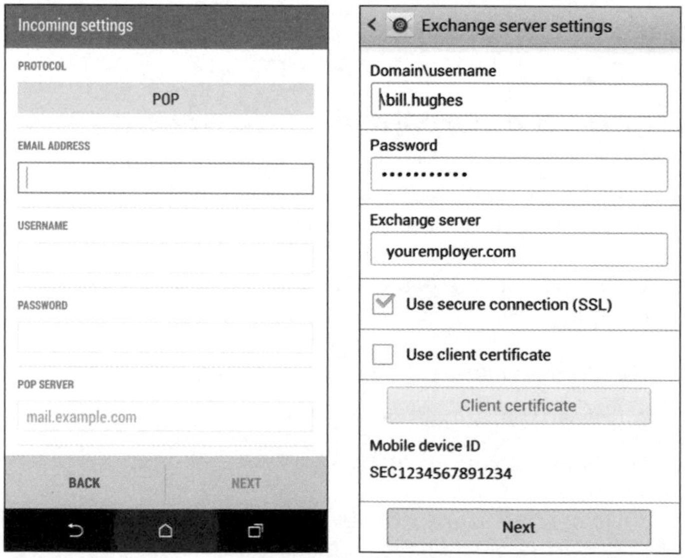

Figure 5-8: The setup screens.

Reading Email on Your Phone

In Figure 5-7, you can see how the email screen looks when you have multiple email accounts. This setup combines all your emails into one inbox. At any given time, you might want to look at the accounts individually or all together.

You'll see your emails in chronological order regardless of which option you choose:

✔ To look at all your emails in one large inbox, tap Combined Inbox. To open any email, just tap it.

✔ To see just emails from one account, tap Combined Inbox (at the top). When you tap it, it shows all the individual email accounts. Tap the account you want to focus on at the moment, and your phone will bring up messages for just that email address.

Writing and Sending an Email

After you set up the receiving part of email, the other important side is composing and sending emails. At any time when you're in an email screen, simply tap the Menu button to get a pop-up screen. From the menu, tap the plus sign.

Here's the logic that determines which email account will send this email:

✔ If you're in an email account's inbox and tap Menu, then the plus sign, your phone sends the email to the intended recipient(s) through that account.

✔ If you're in the combined inbox or some other part of the email app, your phone assumes that you want to send the email from the default email account that you selected when you registered your second (or additional) email account.

When you tap the plus sign in the Menu pop-up menu, it tells you which account it will use. The Email composition screen in Figure 5-9 shows which email account the message will be from.

As shown in this screen, the top has a stalwart To field, where you type the recipient's address. You can also call up your contacts, a group, or your most recent email addresses. (Read all about contacts in Chapter 6.) Tap the address or contact you want, and it populates the To field.

Below that, in the Subject field, is where you enter the email's topic. And below that is the body of the email. There may be a default signature, such as Sent from my HTC One, although your cellular carrier might have customized this signature.

Figure 5-9: The Email composition screen.

At the top of the screen are three icons:

- **Send:** Tap this icon, which looks like an envelope with speed lines trailing it, to send the email to the intended recipient(s).

- **Attach:** Tap this paper-clip icon to attach a file of any variety to your email.

- **Menu:** Tap the three dots to see some less-common options for your email.

The All Draft Items folder, seen in Figure 5-10, works like the Drafts folder in your computer's email program. You access it by tapping the three bars to the left of the email account name. When you want to continue working on a saved email, open the Drafts folder, tap the message, and continue typing.

Icon to access email folders

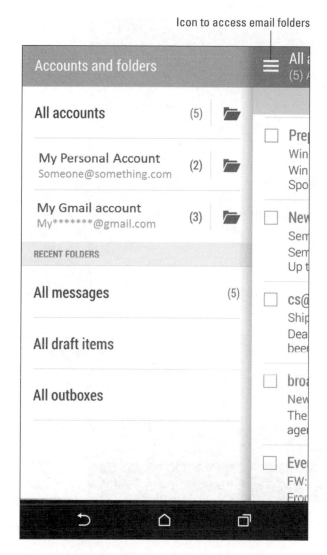

Figure 5-10: Email folders stored on your phone.

Replying to and Forwarding Emails

Replying to or forwarding the emails that you get is a common activity. You can do this from your Email app. Figure 5-11 shows a typical open email.

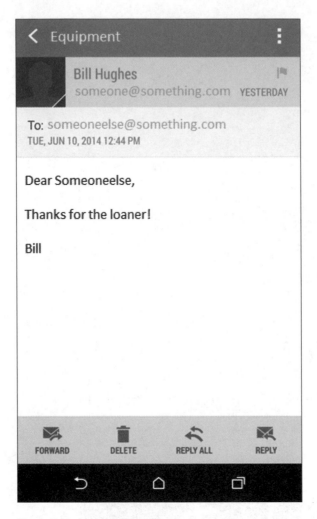

Figure 5-11: An opened email.

1. **Tap the button with the return arrow (at the bottom of the screen).**

   If other people were copied on the email, a single return arrow replies to just the sender; tap the double return arrow to reply to everyone.

   When you tap either of these options, the Reply screen comes back with the To line populated by the sender's email address(es).

2. **Type your comments in the blank space.**

To forward the email, tap the correct menu option of the Device Function keys. After you tap Forward, you enter the address just as you do when sending a new email.

Getting a Grip On Your Contacts

You're probably familiar with using contact databases. Many cellphones automatically create one. You also probably have a file of contacts on your work computer, made up of work email addresses and telephone numbers. And if you have a personal email account, you probably have a contact database of email accounts of friends and family members. If you're kickin' it old school, you might even keep a paper address book with names, addresses, and telephone numbers.

The problem with having all these contact databases is that it's rarely ever as neat and tidy as I've just outlined. A friend might email you at work, so you have her in both your contact databases. Then her email address might change, and you update that information in your personal address book but not in your work one. Before long, you have duplicate and out-of-date contacts, and it's hard to tell which is correct. How you include Facebook or LinkedIn messaging in your contact profile is unclear.

In addition to problems keeping all your contact databases current, it can be a hassle to migrate the database from your old phone. And how should you manage your contacts? This chapter gives you the advantages of each approach so that you can decide which

one will work best for you. That way, you won't have the frustration of wishing you had done it another way before you put 500 of your best friends in the wrong filing system.

Bringing It All Together

Your phone wants you to be able to communicate with everyone you would ever want, in any way you know how to talk to them. This is a tall order, and your HTC One makes it as easy as possible with the contact database application called People. In fact, I wouldn't be surprised if the technology implemented in the People app becomes one of your favorite capabilities on the phone. After all, your HTC One is there to simplify communication with friends, family, and co-workers, and the People application on your phone makes it as easy as technology allows.

At the same time, this information is only as good as your contact database discipline. The focus of this chapter is to help you help your phone help you.

You've started with an empty contact database. You may have been invited to make calls and texts into contacts. In this chapter, I cover how to do that.

Using People

The title "Using People" could be interpreted as a bad habit of a narcissist or sociopath. But in this case, it's a good thing.

And much of the hard work may have already been done if you introduced your phone to your email accounts in Chapter 5. All the contacts from each of your email accounts should be automatically loaded into your People application. You may not have been aware, but you may have already been using People!

Learning to read People

From your Home screen, tap the icon that's shown to the left.

If you haven't created a Gmail account, synced your personal email, or created a contact when you sent a text or made a call, your Contacts list will be empty. If you have done those things, you see a bunch of your contacts now residing on your phone, sorted alphabetically (as shown in Figure 6-1).

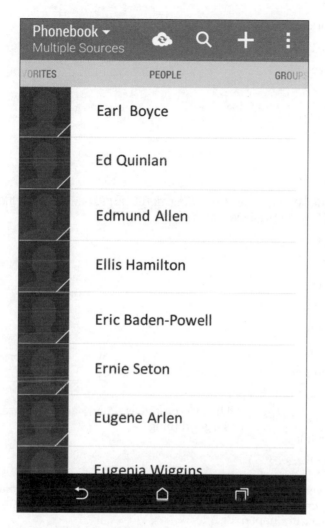

Figure 6-1: The Contacts list.

This database does more than just store names, phone numbers, and email addresses. It can include the following information:

✔ The first and last name of each contact in separate fields

✔ All telephone numbers, including

- Mobile
- Home

- • Work

- • Work fax

- • Pager

- • Other

✔ Email addresses

- • Home

- • Work

- • Mobile

✔ Up to nine IM addresses (including all the largest IM services like Google Talk, AIM, Windows Live, and Yahoo!)

✔ Company

✔ Job Title

✔ Nickname

✔ Mailing addresses

- • Home

- • Work

- • Another location

✔ Any notes about this person

- • Web address

- • Birthday

- • Anniversary

As if all this weren't enough, you can assign a specific ringtone to play when a particular person contacts you. I cover the steps to assign a music file to an individual caller in Chapter 12.

Finally, you can assign a picture for the contact. It can be one out of your Gallery; you can take a new picture; or (as I discuss in Chapter 8) you can connect to a social network like Facebook and use that person's profile picture.

Fortunately, the only essential information is a name. Every other field is optional, and is only displayed if the field contains information to be displayed. Figure 6-2 shows a sparsely populated contact.

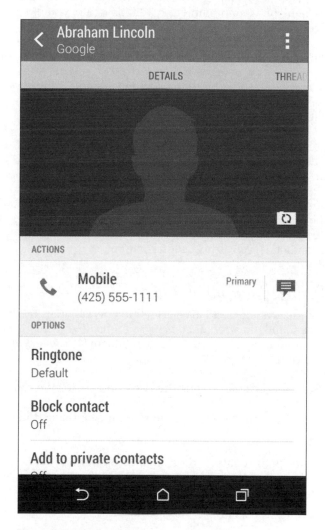

Figure 6-2: A basic contact.

This Contacts list is smart. Allow me to explain some of the things that are going on. Say your best friend is Bill Boyce. You sent Bill a text earlier to let him know about your new phone. You followed the instructions in Chapter 4 and entered his telephone number. You took it to the next step and tapped Add Contact. When you were prompted to add his name, you did. Now your phone has a contact for Bill Boyce.

Then you linked your email. Of course your buddy Bill is in your email Contacts list. So while you were reading this chapter, several things happened. First, your phone and your Gmail account synced. Your phone thinks about it, and figures this must be the same person. It automatically combines all the information in one entry on your phone!

Then your phone automatically updates your Gmail account. If you see the word Google just beneath the email address, this contact is synced with the Gmail account. You didn't have to do anything to make this happen.

Your phone noticed that Bill's work number was in your email contact information, but the mobile phone number you used to text him was not. No problem! Now the contact on your phone includes both the information you had in your email contact as well as his cellular phone.

Linking Contacts on your phone

Now, as slick as this system is, it isn't perfect. If a person goes by different names, you have to link these contacts. For example, if you create a contact for Bill Boyce, but your email refers to him as William D. Boyce, your phone will assume that these are two different people.

No problem. Here are the steps to link the two contacts for the same person:

1. **From one of the contacts, tap the menu icon (the three dots).**

   This brings up the screen shown in Figure 6-3.

   Carefully choose the contact whose name you want to be the primary name. For example, I tapped the link on the William D. Boyce contact. That will be the name used on the combined contact going forward.

2. **Tap the link that says Link.**

   When you tap the link that says Link, your phone will try to help you with some options on where the other contact is stored, such as Facebook, Skype, and LinkedIn.

3. **Tap Other Contacts to link the other contact entry on your phone.**

   Bill Boyce is stored on the phone, so tap the Other contacts.

Figure 6-3: The menu option for Contacts within the People app.

4. Search for the other contacts you wish to link.

Search for Bill Boyce in the text box. It will come up and the two contacts are forever linked, as seen in Figure 6-4.

5. Tap Done.

Let no man put this link asunder. (Unless you made a mistake and want to change it. Then go tap the chain icon to break the link.)

Figure 6-4: The linked contacts.

Linking contacts on your phone and Gmail account

If you created a Gmail account in Chapter 5, realize that your phone and this account automatically share all contact information. This happens without your having to do anything. It just works. When you update your phone, the Gmail account automatically updates. When you update your Gmail account, your phone automatically updates.

In addition to being smart, here are some good reasons to use your Gmail account to store your contact, rather than relying on a database stored solely on your phone:

✔ You don't lose your database if you lose your phone.

✔ If more of your social time is spent on your computer and you use your phone only occasionally, having the most accurate contact database on your computer is probably more valuable.

✔ As nice as the keyboard and screen are on the HTC One, it's easier to make additions, changes, and deletions to a database when you use a full keyboard and large screen. Your choice!

Keep in mind that your phone stores a copy of all contacts in case you're unable to connect to your Gmail account, but the "official" copy of your contacts is stored away from your phone and safely hosted by your friends at Google.

Entering the Contacts on Your SIM card

If your previous phone worked with AT&T or T-Mobile, you probably have a SIM card. Back in Chapter 2, Figure 2-2 shows a profile of SIM cards, although yours probably has the logo of your cellular carrier nicely printed on the card.

While you will someday upgrade your HTC One, your contacts can follow you if you buy a smartphone next time and store them on your email.

Technology's speed

If your cellular carrier was Verizon, Sprint, or U.S. Cellular, you may be confused. Your HTC One has a SIM card. What's the story? These carriers use CDMA technology for voice and for some data features. Up to 3G, the phones using CDMA technology and data services didn't use a SIM card. Today, *all* carriers in the US are implementing a super high-speed data technology called LTE, also called 4G. Because your phone is capable of LTE, you now have a SIM card.

Like many users, you probably have stored your phone contacts on your SIM card. Some GSM-based phones (phones that work on AT&T or T-Mobile networks) allowed you to store your contacts on internal memory within the phone. This allowed you to store more contacts and more information on each contact than you could on the SIM card. However, in most cases, you probably stored your contacts on the SIM card.

This made it easy to switch to a new phone. The SIM card would allow you to bring along your phone account and all your contacts. The good news is that all of us, GSM and CDMA users, can do this with the SIM card. It is not altogether a bad idea to store your contacts on your SIM card if you switch your phone frequently.

I suggest moving them off and putting them with your other contacts. Here is how to do so:

1. **From the Home screen, tap People.**

    You know how to do this.

2. **Tap the Menu key.**

    This brings up all the options for Contacts.

3. **Tap the Manage Contacts option.**

    This brings up the screen in Figure 6-5 with the long list of options.

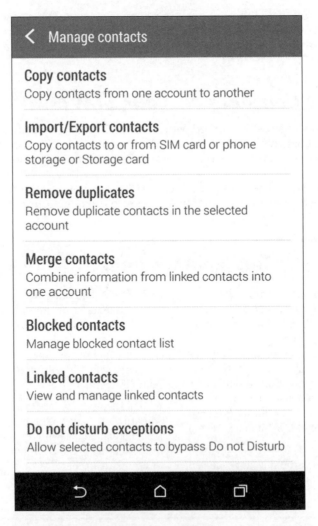

Figure 6-5: The Manage Contacts options.

4. **Tap Import/Export contacts options.**

   Doing so imports this information, and while you do other things, it syncs everything on your phone and then syncs your phone's contacts with those on your Gmail account.

5. **Tap the Import from SIM option.**

   This brings up the screen in Figure 6-6.

Figure 6-6: The Create Contact Under Account options.

6. **Tap Google.**

   You know me. I want you to put these in your Gmail account. Go ahead and tap Google.

Creating Contacts within Your Database

Your phone is out there trying to make itself the ultimate contact database with as little effort on your part as possible. The interesting thing is that the salesperson in the cellular store probably didn't explain this to you in detail. It's a subtle but important capability that's hard to communicate on the sales floor.

Whenever you make or receive a call, send or receive an email, or send or receive a text, your phone looks up the telephone number or email address from which the message originated to check whether it has seen that address before. If it has, it has all the other information on that person ready. If it doesn't recognize the originating telephone number or email, it asks whether you want to make it a contact. What could be easier?

Adding contacts as you communicate

When you get a call, a text, or an email from someone who isn't in your Contacts list, you're given the option to create a profile for that person. The same is true when you initiate contact with someone who isn't in your Contacts list.

When you tap the plus sign (on the right in Figure 6-7), you're immediately given the option to create a contact or update an existing contact. Your phone doesn't know whether this is a new number for an existing contact or a totally new person. Rather than make an assumption (as lesser phones on the market would do), your phone asks you whether you need to create a new profile or add this contact information to an existing profile.

Without Telephone Number   With Telephone Number

Figure 6-7: The dialing screens.

Adding contacts when you're dialing

You can add contacts on the fly:

1. **Tap the phone icon.**

   When you first access the Phone application, it brings up the keypad with a blank screen, as seen in the left screen in Figure 6-7.

2. **Start dialing the number.**

   When you start entering the first number, a pop-up menu asks whether you want to add to your contacts in the People application.

   Be patient. As you continue to type, your phone tries to guess whose name you're typing. Figure 6-8 sees that the digits you have typed are included in the phone number for your good buddy, Robert Baden-Powell. As a courtesy, it tries to offer you a chance to save your tapping finger and just call Robert.

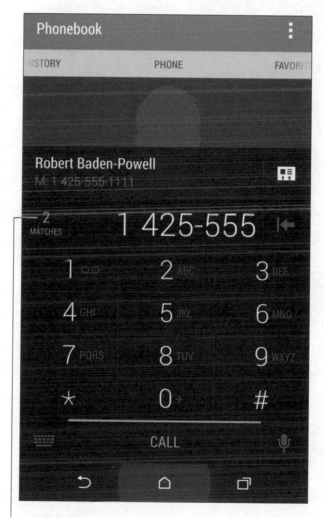

Matches to dialed number

Figure 6-8: The screen as you begin entering the phone number.

If Robert isn't the right person to call, you can see that there are two people with that number sequence in your Contacts list. To call someone else besides Robert, tap the 2 and see the possible contacts.

However, if you're dialing a new number for the first time, just keep on typing. Your phone will take those digits until it no longer recognizes the number. Eventually it gives up on guessing. This is seen in Figure 6-9.

Figure 6-9: You can add a new contact to People when you dial a new number.

3. **When done typing the number, tap Save to People.**

4. **Choose whether this is a new contact or a new number for an existing contact.**

   This brings up the option to save it as a new contact or to add this phone number to an existing contact.

5. **Tap Create Contact.**

   An empty contact profile will give you the option to add a name. Enter as much information on this contact as you want.

6. **Tap Save at the top of the screen.**

   This contact is soon synced with your Gmail account.

Adding contacts manually

Adding contacts manually involves taking an existing contact database and adding its entries to your phone, one profile at a time. (This option, a last resort, was the only option for phones back in the day.)

1. **Tap the people icon.**

   Doing so brings up the list of existing contacts.

2. **Tap the + (plus) sign.**

   A screen with text boxes appears. This is the profile for the contact.

3. **Fill in the information that you want to include.**

   This screen has defaults. For example, it assumes that you want to add the mobile phone number first. If you want to add the work or home number first, tap Mobile to change the field description.

4. **If you want to add a second telephone number, tap the plus sign, and another text box will show up.**

5. **When you're done entering data, tap Save at the top of the screen.**

   The profile is now on your phone. Repeat the process for as many profiles as you want to create.

How Contacts Make Life Easy

After you populate the profiles of dozens or hundreds of contacts, you're rewarded with a great deal of convenience.

Start by tapping a contact. You see that person's profile, as shown in Figure 6-10.

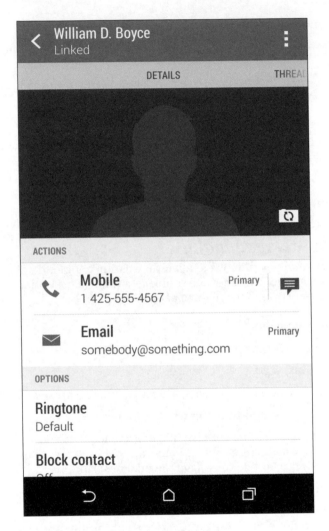

Figure 6-10: A basic contact profile.

All the options you have for contacting this contact are but a simple tap away:

✔ Tap the telephone icon next to the number to dial that number.

✔ Tap the email icon to create an email.

✔ Tap the message balloon icon to send a text.

About the only thing that tapping a data field *won't* do is print an envelope if you tap the mailing address!

Part III
Live on the Internet: Going Mobile

In this part . . .

- Surf the Internet from your phone.
- Get to know Google's Play Store and download exciting new apps to your phone.
- Make browser settings for your favorite websites.

You've Got the Whole (Web) World in Your Hands

In This Chapter

▶ Surfing the Internet from your phone

▶ Setting the browsing settings for you

▶ Visiting websites

*I*f you're like most people, one of the reasons you got a smartphone is because you want Internet access on the go. You don't want to have to wait until you get back to your laptop or desktop to find the information you need online. You want to be able to access the Internet even when you're away from a Wi-Fi hotspot — and that's exactly what you can do with your HTC One. In this chapter, I show you how.

The browser that comes standard with your HTC One works almost identically to the browser that's currently on your PC. You see many familiar toolbars, including the Favorites and search engine. And the mobile version of the browser includes tabs that allow you to open multiple Internet sessions simultaneously.

This chapter goes into much more detail on using the Internet browser on your HTC One, as well as the websites that you can access from your phone. I discuss some of the trade-offs you can make when viewing a web page.

Starting the Browser

To open the browser on your HTC One, tap the Chrome icon on one of the Home screens. Alternatively, tap the application icon and then tap the Chrome icon.

As long as you're connected to the Internet (that is, either near a Wi-Fi hotspot or in an area where you have cellular service), your home page appears. Your default home page could be blank or it could be the Google home page, but most cellular carriers set their phones' home pages to their own websites or to a site selected by them.

If you're out of coverage range, or you turned on Airplane mode (which turns off the cellular and Wi-Fi radios), you get a pop-up screen letting you know that there is no Internet connection. (Read about Airplane mode in Chapter 2.)

Reestablish your connections by pulling down the Notification screen and either tapping the Wi-Fi icon at the top or turning off Airplane mode.

You have three options for getting access to information from the Internet. Which one you use is a personal choice:

- ✓ **Use the regular web page:** In this case you visit the web page via its regular address (URL). The page's text may be small.

- ✓ **Find the mobile web page:** Many websites offer a mobile version of the regular web page. This is an abbreviated version of the full website that you can more easily read on a mobile device.

- ✓ **See if there's a mobile app associated with the web page:** Many websites have found that it's most expedient to write a mobile application to access the information on the website. The app reformats the web page to fit better on a mobile screen — a convenient option if you plan to access this website regularly. I cover this option in detail in Chapter 8.

Accessing Mobile (or Not) Websites

The browser works like the browser on your PC. At any time, you can enter a web address (URL) by tapping the text box at the top of the screen. You can try this by typing in the address of your favorite website and seeing what happens.

For example, the page in Figure 7-1 is the regular version of the website `Refdesk.com`. As you can see, the website is all there. Also as you can see, the text is very small. This particular website is designed to take you to a lot of useful links throughout the Internet, so this is an extreme example of a regular website.

Figure 7-1: The regular and mobile versions of the website Refdesk.com.

You can stretch and pinch to find the information you need. (*Stretching* and *pinching* are hand movements you can use to enlarge/shrink what you see onscreen, as covered in Chapter 2.) With a little bit of practice you can get around on your familiar websites with ease.

The other option is to find the mobile website. The figure on the right in Figure 7-1 shows the mobile version. It has fewer pictures, the text is larger, and the mobile version loads faster — but it's less flashy.

In the case of Refdesk, you can get to the mobile version by entering **m.refdesk.com** into the text block at the top from the software keyboard. Refdesk.com is far from the only website to offer a mobile version. Many sites — from Facebook to Flickr, Gmail to Wikipedia — offer mobile versions.

So how do you get to the mobile websites? If a website has a mobile version, your phone browser will usually bring it up. The most common differences between the address of a mobilized website and a regular one are `.com/mobile` at the end of the address. For example, the mobile version of Amazon.com is `www.amazon.com/mobile`.

If your phone doesn't automatically bring up the mobile version of a site, the simplest way to find it is to Google the desired site along with the term *mobile*. For example, the first option you get from Googling *Flickr mobile* on your phone is the mobilized website for Flickr.

Getting Around in the Browser

When the browser on your phone is active, it should look familiar to your desktop browser. However, some basic icons are missing. To access them, you need to tap the Menu button. This brings up the screen shown in Figure 7-2.

This screen gives you quick access to all your browser screen options. The most import options on the menu include

- **Go forward/backward:** The left and right arrow move you forward and backward in the same way the forward and backward buttons operate on your desktop browser (or on your tape player, if you're still listening to music that way).

- **New Tab:** Tap this to open another tab.

- **New Incognito Tab:** If you want to open a new window, but do it without having your phone tracking what sites you've visited, tap the icon with a silhouette of a person in a trench coat. That brings up an incognito browser session. (Don't tell me why you want to do this. I don't need to know.)

- **Bookmarks:** You can tap the bookmark icon to make this site a favorite. I talk more about bookmarks in the next section.

- **Refresh:** Tap to resend data from the active tab. This is useful if there is no activity for a while. This is the same icon as on your desktop browser with the semicircular arrows chasing each others' tails.

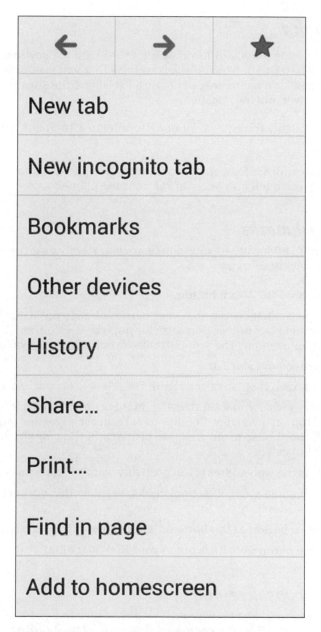

Figure 7-2: The menu options for the Chrome browser.

Using Bookmarks

As convenient as it is to type URLs or search terms with the keyboard, you'll find it's usually faster to bookmark a web address that you visit frequently. Making bookmarks is a handy way to create a list of favorite sites that you want to access over and over again.

A *bookmark* is roughly the equivalent of a Favorite on a Microsoft Internet Explorer browser.

In the next subsections, I tell you how to bookmark a site and add it to your list of favorites. I also tell how you can see your list of bookmarks.

Adding bookmarks

When you want to add a site to your bookmark list, simply visit the website. From there, follow these steps:

1. **Press and hold the Menu button.**

   A menu opens. Chances are that your carrier already put a number of bookmarks on your phone. Some are for popular sites; others help you manage your account. The point is that you can add your own sites.

2. **Tap the grayed-out star icon.**

   You see a screen that looks like Figure 7-3.

   - *Name* is what you want to call it. In this case, the default is Local and National Weather Conditions & Forecast – Weatherbug.com. You can choose to shorten it to just WeatherBug, or anything you want to call it.

   - *URL* is the web address. You probably want to leave this one alone.

   - *Folder* here says mobile bookmarks. I explain this option in the next section.

3. **Tap the Save button at the bottom-right corner of the screen.**

   A thumbnail of the website is put in your Bookmark file.

Bookmark housekeeping

Now that you have added a bookmark, it would be nice to be able to find it. Before we go there, though, wouldn't it be nice if *all* the bookmarks from your browser were to magically appear on your phone? If you use Google's Chrome browser on your PC and signed in with a Gmail account, I have some good news! These bookmarks are already on your phone.

First, I should explain how bookmarks are stored in files on your phone. Then I explain how you access and manage them. This screen in Figure 7-4 shows three folders: Desktop Bookmarks, Other Bookmarks, and Mobile Bookmarks.

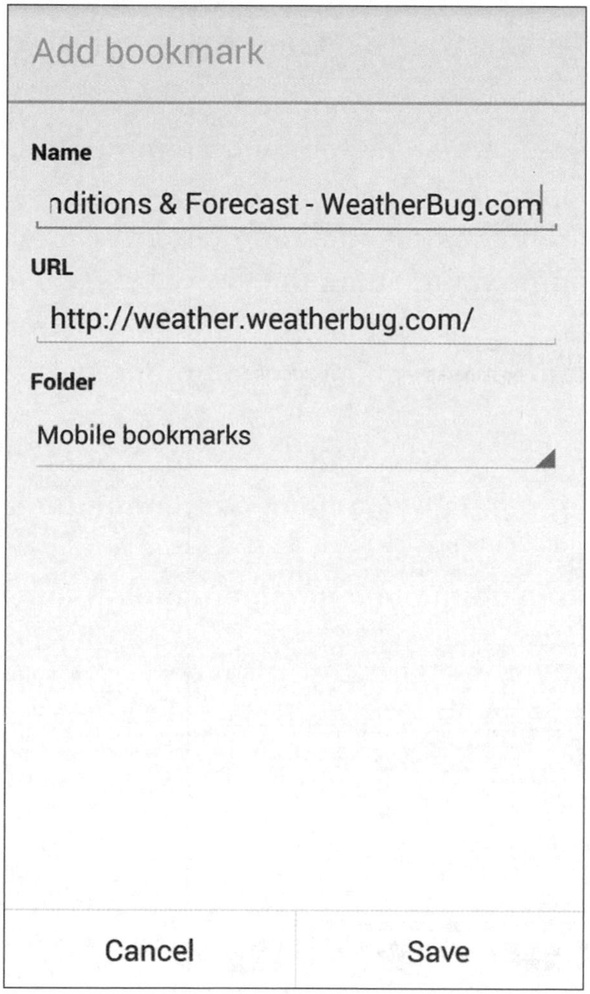

Add bookmark

Name

nditions & Forecast - WeatherBug.com

URL

http://weather.weatherbug.com/

Folder

Mobile bookmarks

Cancel   Save

Figure 7-3: The Add Bookmark screen.

You can find your all bookmarks from the Chrome browser on your PC in the Desktop Bookmarks folder. Just open this file folder and there they are as seen in Figure 7-5.

 If you find a site you like while browsing on your cellphone, you can use it on your desktop too. Figure 7-5 shows the options to saving a bookmark on the Mobile Bookmarks file. Simply change the filing location to Desktop Bookmarks and tap Save. This bookmark you found on your mobile browser will appear on your desktop PC!

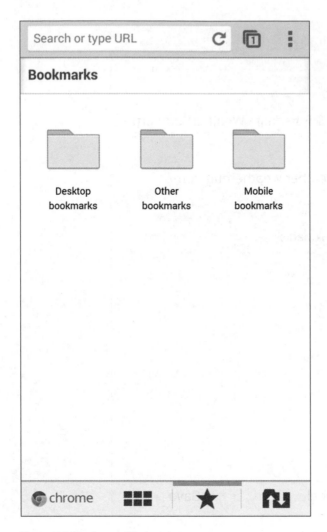

Figure 7-4: Bookmark filing options.

If you open your Mobile Bookmark browser file, you'll see the bookmarks that you have saved. Similarly, the Other Bookmarks file is for bookmarks that you want to save, but don't want to see every time you open your Mobile Bookmarks file.

How do we get to bookmarks? Simple! Bring up the menu that you saw in Figure 7-5 and tap the Bookmarks link. The default is to take you to your Mobile Bookmarks folder. The bookmarks you have saved on your phone will be there. It looks like the layout seen in Figure 7-5.

Link to access bookmark files

Recently closed websites   Bookmarks

Websites that are currently open on your PC

Figure 7-5: Bookmarks file with Desktop bookmarks.

You can get to websites from this screen three ways:

✔ **View Recently Closed Web Site:** When you click this icon (six rectangles), you see *thumbnails* (little bitty pictures) of websites that you recently closed.

✏ **Bookmark Files:** Tap the star icon. This is the active option seen in Figure 7-5. To get to the top file, which is seen in Figure 7-6, tap the link that says Bookmark. This is an active hyperlink that takes you back to the root of the filing system.

✏ **View What Is Currently Open on Your PC:** Are you ready to be blown away? Tap this icon (file folder with up and down arrows) to see the tabs that are currently open on your PC.

Bookmarks are cool and convenient, but you don't always want to save them forever. When a bookmark has served its purpose, rather than have it take up prime real estate on your Bookmarks screen, you can move it or delete it:

1. **Press and hold the website thumbnail.**

2. **Tap Delete Bookmark.**

   Your phone confirms that this is indeed what you want to do.

3. **Tap Yes and the bookmark is gone.**

   On the other hand, if you're unsure, you can just move it to the Other Bookmark file. Tap the Edit Bookmark option, and select the Other Bookmark file to spare its digital existence for another day.

Getting Around in Multiple Browser Sessions

As I mention earlier, it can be convenient to open multiple browser sessions — called *windows* or *tabs* — at the same time. Each window is open to its own website. You can jump around each session with ease, without needing to load a new site each time. To jump among the windows, you tap the tab access icon (highlighted in Figure 7-5).

This has a number on what is supposed to looks like several sheets of paper. The number tells you the how many tabs are active. To jump between sessions, you follow these steps:

1. **Tap the tab access button.**

   This brings up a pop-up screen like that shown in Figure 7-6.

2. **Swipe to the page you want and tap it.**

   The screen becomes full size.

To close a tab, tap the X in the upper-right corner.

Tap to search for images, maps, and more

Figure 7-6: The tab access screen. On your screen, tap the indicated icon to see more.

Googling Your Way to the Information You Need: Mobile Google Searches

When you open the browser, you can use any search engine that you want (for example, Bing or Yahoo!). Still, some functions — web searches and map searches — work especially well when you use the Google search engine.

At the highest level, the search process works just as it does on your PC: You type (or tap) in a search topic, press Enter, and the search engine finds what you're looking for. Depending upon the search engine and your phone, you might have the option of searching by voice.

Android works well with the Google browser primarily because Android was developed by Google.

The HTC One works to make Internet searches more convenient. Three non-descript bars to the left are circled in Figure 7-6. If you tap them, the screen slides to the right to expose Figure 7-7.

These searches are all available on Google, but tapping this button makes it even easier to specifically search for images, videos, maps, and so on.

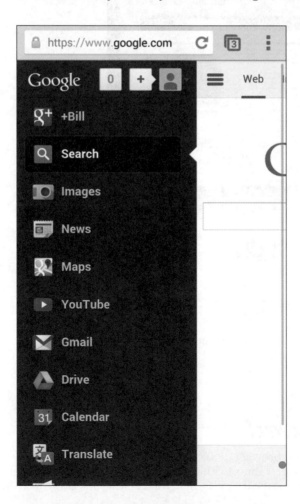

Figure 7-7: The secret Google search icons.

Playing in Google's Play Store

In This Chapter

▶ Getting to know Play Store

▶ Finding Play Store on your phone

▶ Seeing what Play Store has to offer

▶ Downloading and installing Facebook for Android

▶ Rating and uninstalling apps

Most traditional cellphones come with a few simple games and basic applications. Smartphones usually come with better games and applications. For example, your HTC One has a more sophisticated contacts manager, a music app, basic maps, and texting tools. To boot, you can download even better applications and games for phones based on the Google Android platform. Many applications are available for your HTC One, and that number will only grow over time.

Where do you get all these wonderful applications? The main place to get Android apps is the Play Store. You might be happy with the app that came with your phone, but look into the Play Store and you'll find some you never knew you always needed.

In this chapter, I introduce you to the Play Store and give you a taste of what you'll find there. For information on how to buy and download apps, keep reading.

Exploring Your Phone's Mall

The Play Store is set up and run by Google, mainly for people with Android phones. Adding an application to your phone is similar to adding software to your PC. A new application makes you more productive, adds to your convenience, or entertains you for hours on end — sometimes for free. Not a bad deal.

There are some important differences, however, between installing software on a PC and getting an application on a cellphone:

- ✓ **Smartphone applications need to be more stable than computer software because of their greater potential for harm.** If you buy an application for your PC and find that it's unstable (for example, it causes your PC to crash), sure, you'll be upset. If you buy an unstable application for your phone, though, you could run up a huge phone bill or even take down the regional cellphone network. Can you hear me now?

- ✓ **There are multiple smartphone platforms.** These days, it's pretty safe to assume that computer software will run on a PC or a Mac or both. On the other hand, because of the various smartphone platforms out there, different versions within a given platform aren't always compatible. The Play Store ensures that the application you're buying will work with your version of phone.

Getting to the Play Store

You can access the Play Store through your HTC One's Play Store application or through the Internet. I cover both of these methods in this section.

The easiest way to access the Play Store is through the Play Store app on your phone. The icon is at the top of Figure 8-1. To open it, simply tap the icon. When you tap the Play Store icon, you're greeted by the screen shown in Figure 8-1. (If the Play Store app isn't already on your Home screen, you can find it in your applications list.)

As new apps are available, the highlighted apps will change. The Home page changes from one day to the next, but the categories tend to be consistent over time. These categories follow:

- ✓ **Apps:** This showcase highlights valuable applications or games that you might not otherwise come across. This is the first Play Store screen you see (the leftmost screen on the panorama).

- ✓ **Games:** These apps are for fun and enjoyment. As it happens, this is the most-downloaded type of application. Popularity is a good initial indication that an application is worth considering.

Throughout this book, I use the blanket term *applications* or *apps* to refer to games and other kinds of applications. Some purists make a distinction between applications and games. The thing is, from the perspective of a phone user, they're the same: You download an application and use it, whether for fun or to be more productive.

- ✓ **Music:** You can buy your digital music at the Play Store. I talk more about this in Chapter 12.

Figure 8-1: The Play Store.

✔ **Books:** Have you been thinking about getting an e-reader, such as a Nook or a Kindle? Before you spend your hard-earned cash, take a look at the book library here and see whether you like reading on your phone! If you like the way the Nook or the Kindle work, both are available as applications you can download and use to access your accounts on the Barnes & Noble website or Amazon.com.

✔ **Magazines:** Same idea as with books, only these are for periodicals.

✔ **Movies and TV:** As with music, you can download multimedia files and view your favorite movies and TV shows. You can watch them on your HTC One's screen or connect your phone to your HDTV for the big picture. More on this in Chapter 12.

Stocking Your Cart: Shopping for Android Apps

When you head to the local mall with a credit card but without a plan, you're asking for trouble. Anything and everything that tickles your fancy is fair game.

Similarly, before you head to the Play Store, it helps to have a sense of what you're looking for.

The applications for your HTC One phone fall into the following subcategories:

✔ **Games:** Your HTC One takes interactive gaming to a new level. Games in this section of the Play Store fall into the following categories:

   • *Arcade and Action:* Think of games that are based on what you find in arcades — shooting games, racing games, and other games of skill or strategy.

   • *Brain and Puzzle:* Think crossword puzzles, Sudoku, and other word or number games.

   • *Cards and Casino:* Find an electronic version of virtually every card or casino game. (If you know of any game that's missing, let me know so I can write the application and sell it to the three people who play it.)

   • *Casual:* This crossover category includes simpler games, some of which are also arcade, action, or cards, but are distinguished by the ease with which you can pick them up, play them, and then put them down. Solitaire may be the most widespread example of a casual game.

✔ **Applications:** The "non-games" fall into many subcategories:

   • *Comics:* These applications are meant to be humorous. Hopefully, you find something that tickles your funny bone.

   • *Communication:* Yes, the HTC One comes with many communications applications, but these enhance what comes with the phone — for example, tools that automatically send a message if you're running late to a meeting, or text you if your kids leave a defined area.

   • *Demo:* These small, sometimes frivolous, applications don't quite fit anywhere else.

   • *Entertainment:* Not games per se, but these apps are still fun — trivia, horoscopes, and frivolous noisemaking apps. (These also include Chuck Norris "facts." Did you know that Chuck Norris can divide by 0?)

- *Finance:* This is the place to find mobile banking applications and tools to make managing your personal finances easier.

- *Health:* This is a category for all applications related to mobile medical applications, including calorie counters, fitness tracking, and tools that help manage chronic conditions, such as diabetes.

- *Lifestyle:* This category is a catchall for applications that involve recreation or special interests, like philately or bird watching.

- *Maps & Search:* Many applications tell you where you are and how to get to where you want to go. Some are updated with current conditions, and others are based on static maps that use typical travel times.

- *Multimedia:* The HTC One phone comes with the music and video services, but nothing says you have to like them. You might prefer offerings that are set up differently or have a selection of music that isn't available elsewhere.

- *News & Weather:* You find a variety of apps that allow you to drill down till you get just the news or weather that's more relevant to you than what's available on your extended Home screen.

- *Productivity:* These apps are for money management (such as a tip calculator), voice recording, and time management (such as an electronic to-do list).

- *Reference:* These apps include a range of reference books, such as dictionaries and translation guides. Think of this as similar to the reference section of your local library and bookstore.

- *Shopping:* These applications help you with rapid access to mobile shopping sites or do automated comparison shopping.

- *Social:* These are the social networking sites. If you think you know them all, check here just to be sure. Of course, you'll find Facebook, LinkedIn, Twitter, and Pinterest, but you'll also find dozens of other sites that are more narrowly focused and offer applications for the convenience of their users.

- *Sports:* Sports sites to tell you the latest scores and analysis can be found in this part of the Play Store.

- *Themes:* Your phone comes with color schemes, or *themes*. This part of the Play Store offers a broader selection.

- *Tools:* Some of these are widgets that help you with some fun capabilities. Others are more complicated, and help you get more functionality from your phone.

- *Travel:* These apps include handy items such as currency translations and travel guides.

• *Software Libraries:* Computers of all sizes come with software libraries to take care of special functions, such as tools to manage ringtones, track application performance, and protect against *malware* (software that attacks your system or steals your personal information).

Many of your favorite websites are now offering apps that are built for your phone. The previous chapter talks about how you can access websites on your phone. You can use the full site with your high-resolution screen or use the mobile version. A third alternative can be an app that makes the information you want from your phone even easier to access.

Each application category is divided into the following groups:

✔ **Top Paid:** All apps in this category charge a fee.

✔ **Top Grossing:** These are popular and they cost money. This is often a good indication that the app is worthwhile, or at least that it has a crack marketing team. (If the app is not good, the customer comments will show that right away.)

✔ **Top Free:** All apps in this category are the most downloaded apps that you can get free of charge.

✔ **Trending:** These applications are catching on. It's worth considering this category.

✔ **Featured:** These apps are relatively new, and might or might not charge you to download and use them.

In general, you'll probably want to see what you get with a free application before buying one. Many software companies know this, and offer a lower-feature version for free and an enhanced version for a charge. Enjoy the free-market mechanisms on this site and never feel regret for enjoying a free application.

Free applications are great. But don't be afraid of buying any applications that you're going to use frequently. Apps usually cost very little and the extra features may be worth it. Some people (including me) have an irrational resistance to paying $1.99 monthly for something I use all the time. Frankly, this is a little silly. Let's all be rational and be willing to pay a little bit for the services that we use.

Installing and Managing the Facebook for Android App

To make the process of finding and downloading apps less abstract, I show you how to download Facebook for Android as an example.

Downloading the Facebook app

When you want to add a site to your bookmark list, simply visit the site. From there, follow these steps:

1. **Tap the Play Store icon.**

2. **In the Query box, type** Facebook.

   A screen like the one in Figure 8-2 appears.

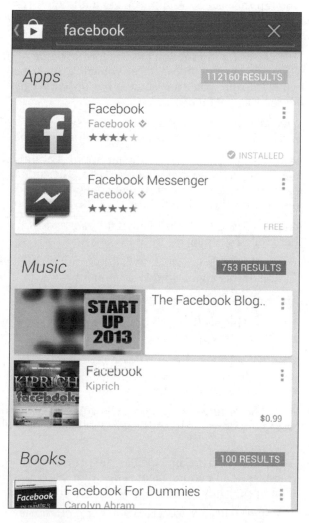

Figure 8-2: The Facebook search results.

3. **Tap the line with the Facebook icon.**

If you tap the line with the Facebook name, it brings up all the titles of apps, games, books, and magazines that include the Facebook name.

As you can see in the search results, several options include the word *Facebook*. The other lines in the Apps section are for apps that include the word *Facebook*. These are typically for apps that "enhance" Facebook in their own ways (as of this writing, 112,160 of them). Rather than go through these one by one, stick with the one with the Facebook icon.

When you tap the Facebook app, you get a lot of information. Before continuing to the next step, I want to point out some important elements on this page:

- *Title Line:* The top section has the formal name of the application with a blue Install button. After you click this to download and install the app, you'll see some other options. I give some examples later in this chapter.

- *Screen Captures:* These representative screens are a little too small to read, but they do add some nice color to the page.

- *Feedback Statistics:* This particular app has about 3.5 stars out of five. That's not bad, but not great. The other numbers tell you how many folks have voted, how many have downloaded this app, the date it was released, and the size of the app in MB.

- *Rate and Review:* This is blank until you've downloaded the app that you'd be voting on.

- *What's New:* This information is important if you have a previous version of this app. Skip this section for now.

- *Description:* This tells you what the app does.

- *Reviews:* This section gets into more details about what people thought of the app beyond the star ranking.

- *More by Facebook:* The app developer in this case is Facebook. If you like the style of a particular developer, this section tells you what other apps that developer offers.

- *Users Also Installed:* Play Store tells you the names of other apps customers downloaded. It's a good indicator of what else you may like.

- *Users Also Viewed:* Same idea as the previous bullet, but it's somewhat less of an endorsement. The other users only looked at these other apps. They didn't necessarily buy them.

- *Developer:* This section gives you contact information for this app's developer.

- *Google Play Content:* This is how you tell the Play Store whether this app is naughty or nice.

4. **Tap the light blue button that says Install.**

Before the download process begins, the Google Play store tells you what this application plans to do on your phone (like in Figure 8-3). This information lists all the permissions you will be granting the application when you download it.

This is similar to the license agreements that you sign. Hopefully you read them all in detail and understand all the implications. In practice, you hope that it's not a problem if lots of other people have accepted these conditions. In the case of a well-known application like Facebook, you're probably safe, but you should be careful with less-popular apps.

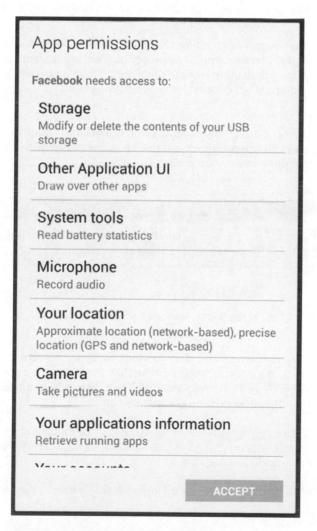

Figure 8-3: The App Permissions screen.

Chapter 1 mentions that you can allow apps to know where you are on a case-by-case basis. Here is where that issue comes up. Each app asks you for permission to access information, such as your location. You may be able to limit the amount of location information. If you're not comfortable with that, you should decline the app entirely.

5. **Tap the light blue Accept button.**

Before the download process starts, your app may want to know two things:

- *Do you want your phone to automatically update when Facebook (or the app provider) releases a newer version?* In general, this is the most convenient option. It's rare, but not unheard of, that an update makes things worse.

- *Do you want to wait for the update to take place only when you have a Wi-Fi connection?* This prevents your phone from downloading a huge application update over the cellular network. In most cases, using a Wi-Fi connection is a better option.

6. **Tap OK.**

This process is like downloading apps to your PC over the Internet. The screens in Figure 8-4 show you the progress of downloading and installing the application.

Download   Installation

Figure 8-4: The Facebook download and installation screens.

This may happen so fast that you look away for a second and when you look back, it's done. Sometimes the Play Store lets you shop while the app downloads in the background. If you like, you can watch the process in the notification portion of your screen.

Apps immediately give you the option to either open them or uninstall them. In this case, the Facebook icon appears on the Apps screen along with some other recently added applications.

If you want this app to be on your Home screen, press and hold the icon.

Creating an account

You can start immediately by tapping Open from the Facebook App screen. You could also tap the Facebook icon from the Apps screen. If you added this app to your Home screen, you can tap its icon there. In any case, opening the app brings up the screen shown in Figure 8-5.

If you don't already have a Facebook account, you can create an account here. Toward the bottom of the screen is the option to sign up for Facebook.

Figure 8-5: The Facebook login screen.

If you already have a Facebook account, enter your email address and Facebook password. Hopefully you can recall your Facebook password. It could be the same as your email password, even though using the same password for multiple accounts is bad security discipline. Obviously, you'll need to get back to your PC to figure out your password if you can't remember it.

To sign up for Facebook, follow these steps:

1. **Enter an email account or cellphone number, as well as a password.**

   See Figure 8-6. After you enter this information, Facebook sends a verification message. If you provide an email address, the app sends you an email. If you use your mobile phone number, it sends you a text. The email or text contains a code.

2. **Enter the code you received.**

   Your Facebook account is validated. To get the most out of Facebook, I recommend *Facebook For Dummies,* 4th Edition by Carolyn Abram.

3. **Choose an option for syncing contacts:**

   • **Sync All:** This option syncs with your existing contacts and makes new contacts for Facebook friends who don't already have an entry in your phone's Contacts database.

   • **Sync with Existing Contacts:** Same idea, but if they don't already have an entry, it doesn't create a new contact.

   • **Don't Sync:** As the name implies, this keeps contacts as contacts and Facebook friends as Facebook friends, and doesn't mix the two.

4. **Tap the word Sync.**

   It's really amazing, all the ways that this information integrates into your phone. Pictures of your contacts start appearing in your Contacts database. You also see (for example) the option to post pictures from your Gallery to your Facebook Page — for openers.

   Within the Facebook app itself, you see the latest posts from your friends in an instant. You get your daily serving of cute kitten images, stories from proud parents about their children, and messages from old flames wondering about what might have been.

Accessing Facebook settings

You can get to the Facebook Settings by tapping the menu button and tapping Settings. I urge you to consider how much you want to control how many of these capabilities you want continuously. Even the most hard-core Facebook fan may need a break from all the notifications.

Figure 8-6: The Sign Up for Facebook screen.

You can get things the way you like in settings, or you can go along with the defaults:

- **Chat Availability:** You can choose to chat or not when you're running this app.

- **Refresh Interval:** You get to decide how often the Facebook app polls the Internet to see whether there are new posts. The default is every hour. Polling more often keeps you better informed, but it can drive up costs. Your choices are shown in Figure 8-7. If you choose Never, it looks for status updates only when you first open the app.

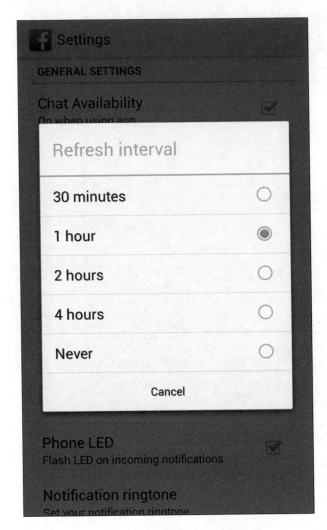

Figure 8-7: The Facebook Refresh Interval options.

✔ **Messenger Location Services:** If you change your mind about having Facebook know where you are, here is how you change the setting.

✔ **Sync Photos:** This option lets you share the images in your Gallery application with Facebook. This is a fun capability, but more than a few people have accidentally posted too many pictures from their phone to their Facebook page. My advice is to be sure that the photo you select in Gallery should be shared — before you share it.

✔ **Notifications:** You can turn off the next bunch of options by deselecting the Notification check box. If you want some but not all, leave the Notification check box selected, and deselect those you don't want.

The next selections offer you various ways you can be notified of a change occurring on your Facebook account.

- *Vibrate:* Every time something happens on Facebook, your phone vibrates.

- *Phone LED:* Every time something happens on Facebook, an LED lights up.

- *Notification Ringtone:* Every time something happens on Facebook, your phone makes a noise. Tap this choice and you see all the options.

These selections let you select which Facebook events trigger a notification alert:

- *Wall Posts*

- *Messages*

- *Comments*

- *Friends Requests*

- *Friend Confirmations*

- *Photo Tags*

- *Event Invites*

- *Application Requests*

- *Groups*

✔ **Sync Contacts:** This option brings back a screen in case you want to change your sync status.

There are lots of combinations and permutations for Facebook. Choose wisely.

Rating and Uninstalling Your Apps

Providing feedback to an application is an important part of maintaining the strength of the Android community. It's your responsibility to rate applications honestly. (Or you can blow it off and just take advantage of the work others have put into the rating system. It's your choice.)

If you want to make your voice heard about an application, here are the steps:

1. **Open the Play Store.**

2. **Tap the three bars to the left of the Play Store icon.**

Doing so brings up a pop-up menu like the one shown in Figure 8-8. This image highlights the three bars in case you are having trouble finding them.

Three bars icon to get pop-up menu

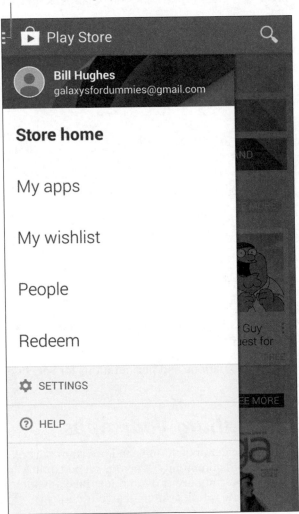

Figure 8-8: The menu from the Play Store.

3. Tap My Apps.

The screen lists all the apps on your phone. Keep on scrolling down. You'll eventually see them all.

4. Tap an app.

If you love the app, rate it highly. You can rank the app and tell the world what you think. See Figure 8-9.

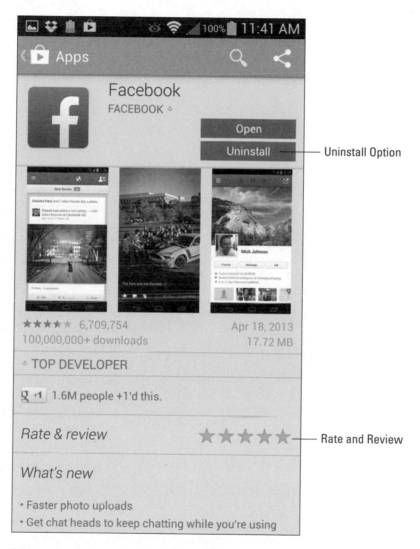

Figure 8-9: The My Apps page for Facebook.

5. Rate it (and if you want to, uninstall it).

If you hate the app, give it one star and blast away. Then you can remove it from your phone by tapping the Uninstall button.

Part IV
Entertainment Applications

Read how to use the Internet radio app Pandora at
www.dummies.com/extras/htconem8.

In this part . . .

- ✔ Take pictures and videos on your phone.
- ✔ Check out the games on the Play Store and download the best ones.
- ✔ Keep track of what you've downloaded.
- ✔ Enjoy a single song, a podcast, or an entire album.
- ✔ Know your licensing options.

Sharing Pictures and Videos

*I*f you're like many cellphone users, you love shooting photographs and videos with your phone. You probably carry your phone with you practically everywhere you go, so you never again have to miss a great photograph because you left your camera at home.

And don't think that HTC skimped on the camera on your HTC One. This camera has lots of shooting options. After shooting them, you can view your shots on that wicked Super AMOLED screen. HTC also includes a Gallery app for organizing and sharing. Plus, the camera can shoot stills *and* video. It would not be surprising if your phone now has more capabilities than your digital camera.

These capabilities actually cause a problem. There are so many options that it can be overwhelming. Research has shown that people fall into one of two categories: The first group tends to use the default settings. If they want to alter the image, they'd prefer to do it on their own PCs. The second group likes to explore all the phone's capabilities. To accommodate both groups of people, this chapter starts with the basics. I cover how to use the camera on your phone, view your pictures, and share them online. This works for everybody. I then focus on the most popular settings for the second.

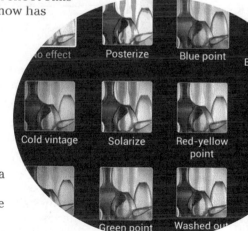

Say Cheese! Taking a Picture with Your Phone

Before you can take a picture, you have to open the Camera app. The easiest way is through the Camera application from the application list. Just tap the camera icon to launch the app. A closely related application on your phone is the Gallery, which is where your phone stores your images. The icons for these two apps are shown in the following figure.

With the Camera app open, you're ready to take a picture within a few seconds. The screen becomes your viewfinder. You'll see a screen like the one shown in Figure 9-1.

Figure 9-1: The screen is the viewfinder for the Camera app.

- How do you snap the picture? Just tap the camera icon on the right (the camera within the oval). The image that's in your viewfinder is what you will see in the digital image.

- Tap the camera icon, and the new picture appears as a thumbnail in the upper right.

- You can tap the thumbnail to take a look, or you can tap again to take another picture. What could be easier?

You probably know that it's not a good idea to touch the lens of a camera. At the same time, it's practically impossible to avoid touching the lenses on your HTC One. This can create a build-up of oil and dirt on your high-resolution lens. Clean your camera lens from time to time. Otherwise your high-resolution images might look like you live in a perpetual fog bank.

Digital magnification

If you want to control how much background you see in your shot, HTC has a slick way to zoom in. When you're using the Camera app, you can use the pinch motion on the screen to zoom in or the stretch motion to pan out.

The viewfinder tells you how much you have zoomed into the shot on the slider icon to the right. Figure 9-2 shows some images that have some and full zoom.

Figure 9-2: The viewfinders when zooming.

Flashing someone

Another important setting you may need to control is the flash. Figure 9-3 shows the icons for each option.

- ✔ Always Flash.
- ✔ Never Flash.
- ✔ Automatic Flash: Let the phone determine if a flash is necessary for a good picture.

Figure 9-3: The flash settings.

As a rule, it is probably best to leave it to the camera's intelligence. However, sometimes a flash isn't allowed or would be rude. In these cases, turn off the flash. Your phone will see if it can make the image work. Just tap the flash icon to change the setting.

You'll have times when you want to force the flash to operate. Let's say Junior is being cute on the playground, but sun is shining. Your camera may say that you don't need a flash, but your head says that you do. You can tell it to flash anyway.

For skeptics only

If you've ever used a camera phone, you might be thinking, "Why make such a big deal about this camera's phone? Camera phones aren't worth the megapixels they're made of." Granted, in the past, many camera phones weren't quite as good as a digital camera, but HTC has addressed these issues with the HTC One.

✔ **Image quality:** The image quality is lower than what you typically get on a dedicated digital camera. The HTC One, however, sports a great deal of processing power to enhance reality and find the best presentation for what is there.

✔ **Photo transfer:** With most camera phones, the photos are hard to move from the camera to a computer. With the HTC One, however (Remember: It uses the Android operating system), you can quickly and easily send an image, or a bunch of images, anywhere you want, easily and wirelessly.

✔ **Screen resolution:** In practice, many camera phone users just end up showing their pictures to friends right on their phones. Many camera phone screens, however, don't have very good resolution. The good news is that the HTC One has a bright, high-resolution screen. Photos look really good on the HD screen.

✔ **Organization:** Most camera phones don't offer much in the way of organization tools. Your images are all just there on your phone, without any structure. But the HTC One has the Gallery application that makes organizing your photos easier. It's also set up to share these photos easily.

Sharing photos right away

After you take a picture, you have a choice. The image is automatically stored in another application: Gallery. This allows you to keep on snapping away and come back to the Gallery when you have time. I cover the Gallery application more in the upcoming section, "Managing Your Photo Images."

However, if you want to send that image right away, here's what you do:

1. **From the viewfinder screen, tap the last image icon.**

   The viewfinder shows a thumbnail of the most recent image you took. This image is at the bottom-right corner of the viewfinder. When you tap that thumbnail, it brings up the image.

2. **Tap the Image.**

   Anywhere on the screen will do. This brings up the current image as seen in Figure 9-4. It also brings up some options. Right now, you're interested in sharing.

3. **Tap the share icon.**

   You see options to forward the image, although your phone might not support all the options listed here:

   • *Facebook:* In Chapter 8, I cover how to connect your phone with Facebook. You can take a picture and post it on your Facebook account with this option. This option appears only after you download the Facebook app and register.

   • *Scribble:* You can take the image and draw on it.

   • *Messaging or Message+:* Attach the image to a text message to someone's phone.

   • *Drive, Dropbox, or Cloud:* Upload the image to your favorite server that resides in the cloud (so it's saved elsewhere than just on your cellphone).

   • *Email or Gmail:* Send the image as an attachment with your main email account. If that's Gmail, this option and the Email option are the same. If not, this selects Gmail.

   • *Bluetooth:* Send images to devices, such as a laptop or phone, linked with a Bluetooth connection.

   • *Picasa:* This Google website helps its subscribers organize and share photos. The main advantage for subscribers is that they can send links to friends or family, rather than send a lot of high-resolution files. Read more on Picasa in the next section.

   • *Google+:* This social networking site is second in popularity only to Facebook. If you signed up for Google+ when you connected your phone, you can use this service to host images immediately.

● *Hangouts:* This image-oriented social network, from Google, allows you to chat and share images.

● *Photos:* This app is similar to the Gallery. If you try Photos and like it better, go for it.

When you select one of these options, the image is automatically attached or uploaded, depending upon the nature of the service you selected. If one of these options doesn't quite suit your need to share your pictures, perhaps you're being too picky!

Figure 9-4: A recent image in the Gallery.

Of course, an account with Gmail (that is, an email address that ends in @ gmail.com) is entirely optional. However, there are advantages to having a Gmail account with your Android-based HTC One phone: For example, you automatically become a subscriber to Picasa and other Google-owned services.

Getting a Little Fancier with Your Camera

By just using the options on the viewfinder, you can have a great time snapping good-looking pictures that are surprisingly easy to either view on your phone or send to someone else.

I can't cover everything about settings. As much as I would like to, it would be impossible to cover all the combinations. In my count, there are 2.43 billion possible combinations of filters, lighting, and modes. If you were to start now and take a picture every 10 seconds, you would not run out of combinations for over 700 years. Realistically, neither you nor your phone will last that long.

If you want to get a little fancier, tap the three vertical dots in the lower-left corner (the menu icon). The viewfinder displays some nice, simple options seen in Figure 9-5 for your basic photography:

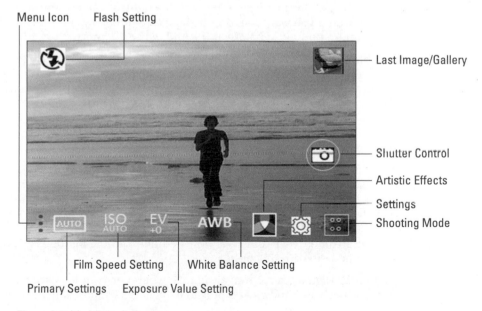

Figure 9-5: It's a little darkroom on your camera.

- **Main Settings:** This icon, the box that says Auto, lets you choose some options to get better pictures. This includes settings for portraits, landscapes, nighttime images, and macro (closeup) shots. Because these are so useful, I describe them more in the next section.

- **Film Speed (ISO) Setting:** This is a hold-over from the days of analog cameras and film. Photographers bought film types to meet the kind of lighting. There was "fast" film for dim lighting or "slow" film for better detail during good lighting. Generally, a setting of 100 was slow and a setting of 400 was fast. For most cases, just leave this setting at Auto.

- **Exposure Value (EV):** This setting lets you darken or brighten up your images. The range is between -2.0 and +2.0, where -2.0 is noticeably darker and +2.0 is noticeably brighter. It is easiest to use the 0 setting and let the camera set the best brightness.

- **White Balance:** Your camera can compensate for different lighting sources. Compared to direct sunlight, fluorescent lights tend to add a green or blue tint. The AWB (automatic white balance) setting can figure out the lighting conditions and make the whites look more white (versus gray or yellowish). Alternatively, you can tap this icon and set white balance manually.

- **Artistic Effects:** This icon lets you apply digital filters for artistic effect. I cover these in more detail later. Keep in mind that you can take a normal picture and add these filters later.

- **Settings:** This is the icon to get to the control camera settings, such as where you want to store the images in memory, and the nitty-gritty camera options I explore at the end of the chapter.

- **Shooting Mode:** Sure you can add effects later, but HDR (high dynamic range) is cool in many circumstances and deserves to be on the viewfinder. HDR automatically enhances the color in the photo. Usually, this is great. Other times, like in low light, it is a waste of time.

Making a scene selection

If you're taking a still image of your friends at the park, your HTC One default settings will work well. To save you from having to make dozens of adjustments, HTC offers a number of scenarios and makes the most important settings to offer the best chance for a good image. These scenarios include:

- **Nighttime:** You're out past your bedtime and the lighting is dark. Get some help with this option.

- **HDR:** High dynamic range will take whatever your lens sees and make it look brighter and clearer. It is like magic! Try it and see for yourself.

- **Sweep Panorama:** Take a wider shot than you can with a single shot. Press the camera button while you rotate through your desired field of view. The application stitches the individual photos into a single wide-angle shot.

- **AntiShake:** This option compensates for most shaking mitts. If too much caffeine is causing your shots to blur, this is your answer.

- **Manual (M):** This gets you to the camera settings.

- **Portrait:** This mode automatically hides subtle facial imperfections. (No guarantees!) The good news is that when you use the front-facing camera for a *selfie* (a shot you take of yourself, while you're holding the phone), the camera uses this setting as the default. Users of a certain age will appreciate any help we can get.

- **Landscape:** This is the choice if you want to take a distant shot.

- **Backlight:** If you have to take a shot towards the sun or a bright light, use this setting to compensate the best way possible.

- **Text:** Use this setting if you're an international spy and are stealing the top secret plans from the enemy. It also works to take images of books and reports.

- **Macro:** Sometimes you want to take an image of a small object up close. This is the setting for you.

The scene selections make it easy to get better-than-average images with just a few quick clicks.

Shooting mode setting

The next settings option for the average user is the shooting modes. Tapping this icon brings up the options shown in Figure 9-6. When you tap an option, it's circled in bright orange:

- **Camera:** This implies using the camera lens on the back of your phone with all the great features we have covered so far in this chapter.

- **Video:** This is the icon you use to switch to the video camera on your phone. More on that later in this chapter.

- **Zoe Camera:** This is a hybrid between the camera and the video recorder. Its primary purpose is to use the smarts and the inexpensive storage in your camera/phone to help you capture the perfect shot by taking a very fast series of still shots that is not quite a video so you can select the exact image when everything is perfect.

✓ **Selfie:** This option uses the front-facing camera so you can see yourself on the screen. Its default is to give you a few seconds of delay so you can get your hand away from the lens once you tap the shutter!

✓ **Dual Capture:** You have two cameras on your phone. One is facing out the back and the other is forward facing. This mode lets you take pictures from both at the same time.

✓ **Pan 360:** This option lets you spin in place to take an image a full 360 degrees around.

Figure 9-6: The mode options on the camera viewfinder.

Settings for the rookie

You may want to control these options even if you aren't a camera expert. Tapping the settings icon on the viewfinder brings up a number of choices:

✓ **Storage options:** You have two memory options as discussed back in Chapter 2: the built-in memory and your removable SD card. In general, it is better to store your images on the SD card. If you prefer to store it on the phone, you can choose that option here.

✓ **Review Duration:** If you like to see the shot immediately after you snap it, the camera can show it to you for a few seconds.

✓ **Continuous shooting:** This option lets you take three shots per second by holding down the shutter. If your subject is prone to blinking at just the wrong moment, a series increases the chance of getting a good shot. The phone will present the series right away so you can see whether any of them were good. You can go back and pick your favorite of the bunch and delete the rest. This is another option to the Zoe setting described earlier. This also works well for action.

✔ **Volume button option:** The volume button on your phone can be called to help with your photography. If you want, you can tap the volume button to snap a picture (instead of tapping the shutter icon). You could also set the up volume button to zoom in and the down volume button to pan out. The third option is to have the volume button do nothing but adjust the volume.

Advanced settings and effects options

This chapter covers a great number of options. However, some Dummies want to have complete control of everything. This section is for you, type As.

✔ **Manual Settings:** In the Primary settings, you have the Manual Option. This lets you go in and set the digital equivalent of the film speed, the exposure value, and focus zone.

✔ **Filters:** The HTC One offers you a lot of cool filters. From the view-finder, tap the filter icon to bring up a panorama of choices like those in Figure 9-7. Have fun!

Figure 9-7: The filter options on the camera viewfinder.

🖊 **Make-Up Level:** When you tap the setting icon, you are given the option to set the make-up level from 0 to 10. The issue is that digital cameras can sometimes be too good, and can exaggerate facial imperfections. (I mention this issue earlier when talking about portrait mode.) This setting lets you control how much "help" is offered to blur skin imperfections while retaining high resolution of features.

🖊 **Image Adjustments:** Here you can get to the nitty-gritty of how the image will look using settings for contrast, saturation, and sharpness. Figure 9-8 shows the range of settings you can manipulate.

🖊 **Crop:** The default on your camera is a wide setting with a 16:9 ratio of width to height. You can also set it to the more traditional 4:3 ratio. If you want to be creative, you can make it square (which is a 1:1 ratio).

🖊 **Guide Lines:** If your photos are kittywampus or cockeyed much of the time, you can have lines help you get your vertical and horizontals lined up.

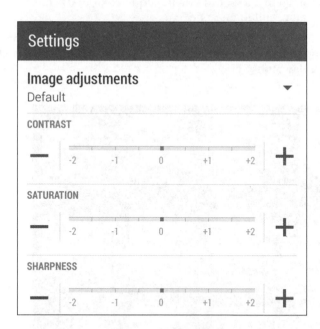

Figure 9-8: The image adjustments options.

These modes help when you're taking the shot. You can also edit an image later. It's easier to do complicated image editing on your desktop computer instead of your phone. However, you can make some edits on your phone and send your photo off right away. It's your choice.

The Digital Camcorder in Your Pocket

Your HTC One Camera application can also function as a digital camcorder.

Starting the camcorder

All you need to do is to put your camera into Camcorder mode: Tap the shooting mode icon on the camera viewfinder and tap the video icon. Poof! You switch from photographer to videographer.

At this point, recording video starts when you push the video camera silhouette. (This is where the shutter icon for the camera used to be.) You get the notification that says Rec in red and the timer from when it started. The recording continues until you either tap the stop button (the circle with the white square in the center on the right side of the viewfinder) or the pause button (the parallel slashes in the middle). See Figure 9-9.

Pause Button

Record Button

Switch back to camera Button

Figure 9-9: Your phone's camcorder viewfinder.

You can tap the lower button to switch back to the camera. Your other option is to tap the button with the red dot to begin recording again.

Your phone is not only recording the video, but it's also recording the sound. Be careful what you say!

Taking and sharing videos with your camcorder

Just as you share photos you take with the camera, you can immediately share, play, or delete a video by tapping the video viewer. Also, the video is immediately saved on your camera. It's stored in the Gallery app (described earlier in this chapter), but you can see it from your Video Player app (covered in Chapter 12).

You can get fancy with some of your camcorder settings, but you won't find nearly as many settings as you have for your camera — fortunately! In addition to the familiar exposure settings, you can adjust video primary settings and camera settings. By tapping the primary settings you have the option of:

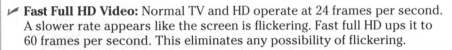

 ✔ **Standard Video:** This setting takes 24 frames per second images at the resolution set within video settings. Use this setting most of the time.

 ✔ **Slow Motion Video:** Here you can get fancy and take a slow motion video.

 ✔ **Fast Full HD Video:** Normal TV and HD operate at 24 frames per second. A slower rate appears like the screen is flickering. Fast full HD ups it to 60 frames per second. This eliminates any possibility of flickering.

 ✔ **Video HDR (Full HD):** If you like the colors associated with the HDR setting on your still images, you can get them with video on this setting.

You can also tap the settings icon when you're in video mode. The important setting is the resolution. The options are seen in Figure 9-10.

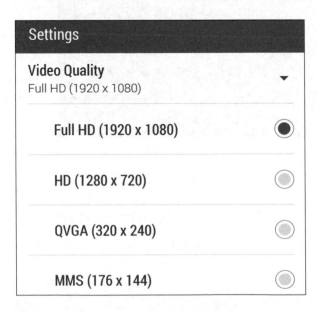

Figure 9-10: The camcorder resolution options.

There is a legitimate question about what video size (resolution) you should use. The default option, 1920×1080, is the resolution on full HD TVs.

You may have noticed that many TVs call themselves HD TVs, then refer to being 720P or 1080i. Rather than get into this issue, you are probably fine at the default full HD resolution. To put this in perspective, a 32GB memory card, a reasonable size card that is in the $20 range, could record in the range of 5 hours of full HD video.

The lowest resolution is 176 by 144. This is okay resolution for a small video image on a web page. Using this setting, you could take 80 hours of video on that 32GB memory card, but it would be very disappointing in any other setting besides a web page. You can readily show a higher resolution video on a screen that has lower resolution. You cannot make a lower resolution video look any better on a higher resolution screen. It is a good idea to use a higher resolution than you think you need.

Your phone can handle up to a 128GB card. These are just now starting to be available in the $150 range.

Managing Your Photo Images

After you take some great pictures, you need to figure out what to do with them. Earlier in this chapter, I describe how to send an image immediately to another site or via email. Doing those things with pictures isn't so common, though. In most cases, it's easier to keep on doing what you were doing and go back to the Gallery application when you have some time to take a look.

Your choices include

- Store them on your phone within the Gallery app.
- Transfer them to your PC to your photo album application by sending them with email.
- Store them on an Internet site, like Picasa or Flickr.
- Print them from your PC.
- Email or text them to your friends and family
- Any combination of the preceding choices.

This section covers how to do each of these options.

Unlike many regular cellphones with a built-in camera, the HTC One makes it easy to access these choices. You need to determine the approach(es) you want to take to keep your images when you want them to stick around. The rest of this chapter goes through your options.

Even though the Camera and Gallery apps are closely related, they're separate.

The Gallery's main screen (shown in Figure 9-11) shows how the app first sorts the images on your phone by time, depending upon when they originated.

Figure 9-11: The Gallery app.

All your photos from the Camera app are placed in Gallery. The application groups pictures or videos taken about the same time, and sorts them based upon the time division that works for you. If you tap the Gallery link, the app sorts your images by year, month, day, or event.

Using Images on Your Phone

Besides sharing photos from your camera, your HTC One phone allows you to use a Gallery photo as wallpaper or as a contact photo. And if the fancy settings in the Camera application aren't enough, you can wrangle minor edits — as in cropping or rotating — when you have an image in Gallery. See Figure 9-12.

Figure 9-12: Choose from menu options in Gallery.

The first step is to find the image that you want in Gallery. If you want to do something to this image other than send it, press and hold the menu button at the bottom-left corner of the screen.

- **Edit:** If you're disappointed that you didn't use some of the advanced settings in camera, relax. You can use this option to get creative with the image you select. All the options that overwhelmed you are here again!

- **More Info:** See the information on the image: its *metadata,* which is fixed and cannot change. This includes the location of the shot, when it was made, the camera type, and a bunch of other details.

- **Copy to Clipboard:** Copy a version of the image to be pasted into another application.

- **Rotate Left/Rotate Right:** Flip the image one way or the other.

- **Crop:** Cut away unnecessary or distracting parts of the image. The application creates a virtual box around what it considers to be the main object. You can move the box around the image, but you can't resize it. You then can either save this cropped image or discard.

- **Rename:** Change the cryptic number automatically assigned to your image to a more meaningful description.

- **Slide Show:** This displays each of the images for a few seconds. You can not only set the speed for transition, but also add music and select among several image transitions.

- **Set As:** Make this image your wallpaper or set it as the image for a contact.

Deleting an image

Not all the images on your phone are keepers. This is particularly true if you're using the Continuous option to take a quick series of images.

When you want to get rid of an image, do this:

1. **Press and hold the image you want to delete.**

   In a second, an icon appears at the top of the screen in the shape of a trash can.

2. **If you want to delete this image, tap Delete.**

   The camera verifies that this is your intent. After you confirm, the image goes away.

When I say that the photos you delete are gone forever, I do mean *for-ev-er.* Most of us have inadvertently deleted the only copy of an image from a PC or a digital camera. That's not a pleasant feeling, so be careful.

Viewing images on your phone

The HD screen on your HTC One is a great way to enjoy your photos and share them with family and friends. Depending upon the circumstances, you can view images one at time or as a slide show.

To see one image at a time, just tap that image. See a series of images by tapping Slide Show, which brings up the next image in chronological order, every four seconds. The slide show icon is at the top of the image you're viewing.

Sharing Your Photos

Organizing your photos into albums is important. After you've been taking photos for a while, the job of organizing gets more difficult. You can't remember whether that picture of Johnny was from spring break or Easter. Start putting your pictures in albums sooner rather than later!

You can try to do this in the Gallery, but unfortunately, Gallery isn't really set up to handle your entire photo library.

You have a number of options to get the photos off your phone so you can sort, edit, and organize them. I discuss how to do this with a single image at the beginning of the chapter. It's straightforward to do this with multiple images from within a given folder from the Gallery application.

When you tap Share, the pop-up for the Share options appears (see Figure 9-4). From this pop-up, you select your sharing option. The multiple images are all handled in one group. *Note:* This is the same list of sharing options you have for a single photo or video.

As I mention earlier, there is much to be said about storing your digital images on the Internet at an image hosting site like Picasa. If you have a Gmail account, you already have a Picasa account. If not, just register with Picasa at http://picasa.google.com.

Picasa isn't the only image-hosting site on the block. Flickr and Windows Live Photo Gallery are also available, to name a few. The advantage of using Picasa is that because the Android operating system and Picasa are both owned by Google, Picasa is already integrated into the system. It's not heroic to use the other sites, but that discussion goes beyond the scope of this book.

The advantages of using Picasa include

- ✔ **The storage capacity is huge.** You might have a large memory card in your phone, but the storage available on any image-hosting site will dwarf what you have.

  When you upload to Picasa, a copy of the images remains on your phone. You might want to keep it there, or you might want to delete it after you transferred the images successfully to make more room on your phone.

- ✔ **It's professionally backed up.** How many of us have lost photos? How many of us have lost phones? 'Nuff said.

- ✔ **Picasa is free.** Google offers this service at no charge.

- ✔ **Access your images wherever you have Internet access.** Although showing pictures on your phone is great, Gallery isn't set up to host your complete photo library. Picasa is.

- ✔ **Others can see your images with links.** Rather than sending all 25 16MB image of your kids at the birthday party, just send the link. Granny might want all the shots in high resolution. Your college roommate probably is fine with the low-resolution images on the Picasa site. No need to clog your old pal's inbox (unless you want to).

- ✔ **You control who has access.** Picasa allows you to set up access to selected groups. You can set it so that family has more access than your co-workers, for example.

- ✔ **You can order prints from your PC.** No need to transfer the images to another storage medium and then trudge down to a store to get prints.

- ✔ **There are tools to help you sort your images.** Gallery has limited control over your folders. With Picasa you can get fancy, or you can keep it very simple. Your choice.

Saving to Picasa is easier than sending an email if you have a Gmail account. Tap the Picasa sharing option, and it will upload that image. You can now create a folder to store the image, edit the image, or share it on other web services. All this is as easy as pie!

Playing Games

In This Chapter

▶ Perusing the games available on the Play Store

▶ Downloading games to your phone

▶ Keeping track of what you've downloaded

Games are the most popular kind of download for smartphones of all kinds. In spite of the focus on business productivity, socializing, and making your life simpler, games outpace all other app downloads. The electronic gaming industry has larger revenues than the movie industry — and has for several years!

The fact of the matter is that your HTC One, with its large screen, makes Android-based games more fun. And because you already have it, maybe you should take a break and concentrate on having fun!

Categorizing Games

The Games category of Play Store (shown in Figure 10-1) is huge, and it includes everything from simple puzzles to simulated violence. All games involve various combinations of intellect, skill (either cognitive or motor), and role-playing.

We could have a lively and intellectually stimulating debate on the merits of games versus applications.

Games

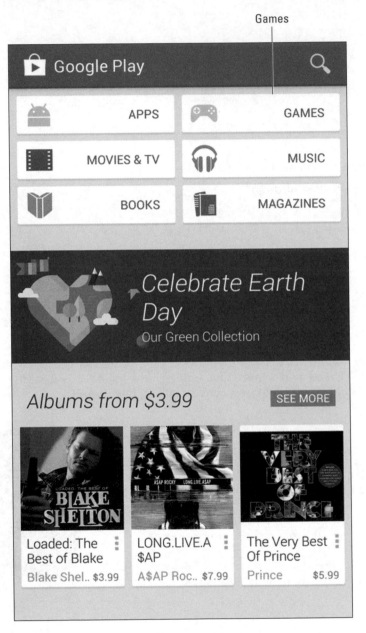

Figure 10-1: The Games button on the Play Store screen.

For the purposes of this book, the differences between games and apps are as follows:

- Apps and Games are different sections of the Play Store.

- If a person likes a game, he or she tends to play it for a while, maybe for a few weeks or even months, and then stop using it. A person who likes an app tends to keep on using it.

- People who use their phones for games tend to try a wide range of games.

For these reasons, I will pick up where I left off in Chapter 8 and expand on some elements of the Google Play store that are relevant for gamers.

The Games home tab

When you tap the Games option shown in Figure 10-1, you go to the home tab for Games. If you scroll down, you see many suggested games. An example of this is shown in panorama in Figure 10-2. If you aren't sure what games you might like to try, don't worry: You have lots of options. The options shown in Figure 10-2 will probably be different from those you will see. These categories are regularly updated with the latest games.

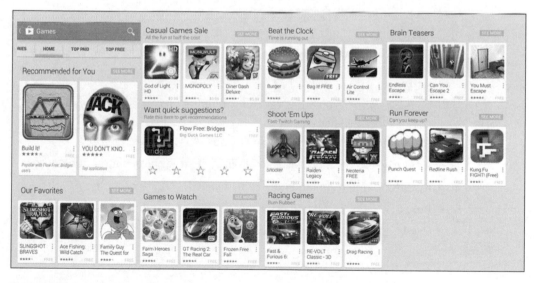

Figure 10-2: The Games home tab.

The Categories tab

If you scroll to the left from the tab that says Home, you see a tab for Categories. These are seen in Figure 10-3.

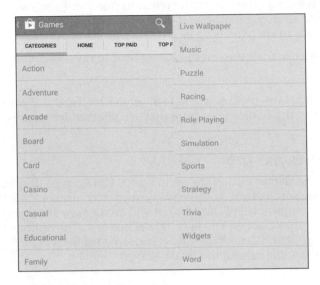

Figure 10-3: The Games categories tab.

In the Play Store, Games are divided into the following genres and sub-genres:

- **Action.**

  - *Shooting:* Projectiles range from bullets to marshmallows to antiballistic missiles.

  - *Fighting:* Fighting (combat) games vary by level of gore.

- **Adventure.** This includes role playing, strategy, and simulation genres.

- **Arcade.** Game room and bar favorites.

- **Board.** Versions of familiar (and some not-so-familiar) board games.

- **Cards.** Every card game you can imagine.

✔ **Casino.** Simulations of gambling games; no real money.

✔ **Casual.** Games that you can easily pick up and put aside.

✔ **Educational.** Enjoyable games that also offer users enhanced skills or information.

✔ **Family.** A variety of game genres that is all G-rated.

✔ **Live Wallpaper.** These include many games from the other categories, but with the feature that you set them as your wallpaper.

✔ **Music.** These games all include music in some way.

✔ **Puzzles.** This genre includes games like Sudoku or Flow Free.

✔ **Racing.** Cars, go-karts, snowboards, jet skis, biplanes, jets, or spacecraft competing with one another.

✔ **Role Playing.** If reality isn't your thing, you can enjoy another world created by the author of a game.

✔ **Simulation.** If reality isn't your thing, and you don't want a reality created by some author, you can create your own reality.

✔ **Sports Games.** Electronic interpretations of real-world activities that incorporate some of the skill or strategy elements of the original game; vary based upon the level of detail.

✔ **Strategy.** These games emphasize decision-making skills, like chess; a variety of games with varying levels of complexity and agreement with reality.

✔ **Trivia.** If you like Trivial Pursuit, this is the genre for you.

✔ **Widgets.** These are the games that automatically appear on your home screen, like everyone's favorite, Tic-Tac-Toe.

✔ **Word.** These games include words such as Scrabble, crossword puzzles, and Jumble.

Many games appear in more than one category, particularly the ones that are in Live Wallpaper and Widgets.

Each game has a description page. It's similar to the description page for apps, but it emphasizes different attributes. Figure 10-4 is an example Description page.

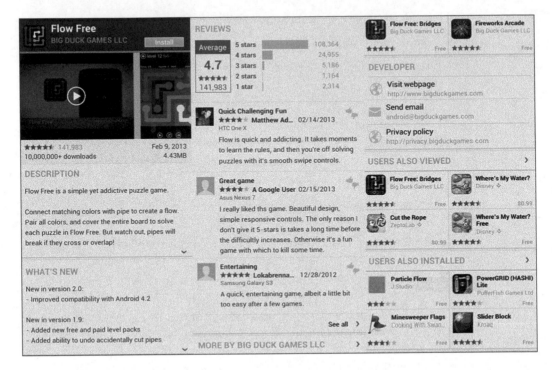

Figure 10-4: A description for Flow Free.

When you're in a category that looks promising, look for these road signs to help you check out and narrow your choices among similar titles:

- **Ratings/comments:** Gamers love to exalt good games and bash bad ones. The comments here are complimentary, and the overall ranking next to the game name at the top suggests that many others are favorable.

- **Description:** This tells you the basic idea behind the game.

- **What's New:** This section tells what has been added since the previous release. This is relevant if you have an earlier version of this game.

- **Reviews:** Here is where existing users get to vent their spleen if they do not like the game, or brag about how smart they are for buying it ahead of you. The comments are anonymous, include the date the comment was left, and tell you the kind of device the commenter used. There can be applications that lag on some older devices. However, you have the HTC One, which has the best of everything (for now).

- **More Games by Developer:** If you have a positive experience with a given game, you may want to check that developer's other games. The More Games by section makes it easier to find these other titles.

- **Users Also Viewed/Users Also Installed:** This shows you the other apps that other people who downloaded this app have viewed or downloaded. These are some apps that you may want to check out.

- **Price:** As a tie-breaker among similar titles, a slightly higher price is a final indication of a superior game. And because you're only talking a few pennies, price isn't usually a big deal.

Leaving Feedback on Games

For applications in general, and games in particular, the Play Store is a free market. When you come in to the Play Store, your best path to finding a good purchase is to read the reviews of those who have gone before you.

Although more than a million users have commented on Angry Birds, most games do not have that kind of following. One could argue that your opinion would not move the overall rating for a frequently reviewed game like Angry Birds. You can't say the same for other games.

One of the suggestions from Figure 10-2 is the game World of Thingies. The game description for one of the games, Zombro, is seen in Figure 10-5.

A description page, before you download it to your phone, will have the Install option; the feedback areas is grayed out. The description page *after* you download it to your phone will offer Open and Uninstall options, and the feedback areas are active.

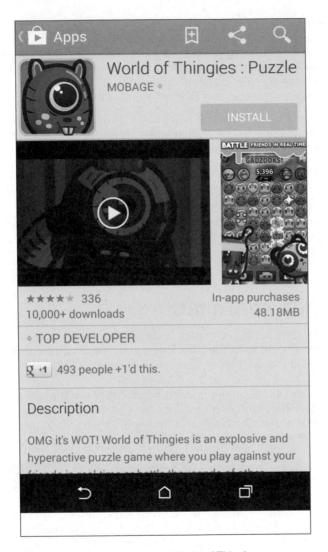

Figure 10-5: The description for World of Thingies.

As of this writing, World of Thingies has been reviewed by 336 gamers. Your opinion matters more for this game than for the heavily reviewed games. After you've downloaded and played a game, you can help make the system work by providing your own review. This section reviews the process, starting at the first screen of the Play Store.

1. **Tap the three bar icon to the left of the Play Store logo.**

   This brings up a menu.

2. **Tap My Apps.**

   This brings up the applications that you've downloaded. The Play Store does not distinguish between games and apps. They're all in the same list.

3. **Tap the game for which you'd like to leave feedback.**

   Tapping the title of the game normally brings up a game description. After you've downloaded a game, however, a Rate & Review section lets you leave feedback.

4. **Tap the stars on the screen.**

   This brings up another screen.

5. **Tap the number of stars that you believe this game deserves.**

   You then make a name for yourself and enter any comments. See Figure 10-6. You cannot enter comments without first choosing the number of stars for this game.

6. **When you're done, tap OK.**

   Your comments are sent to the Play Store for everyone to see. For the sake of the system, make sure that your comments are accurate!

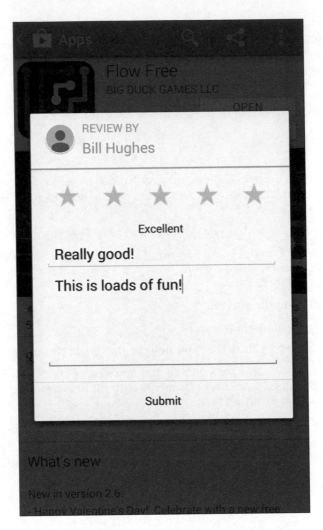

Figure 10-6: The ratings screen after entering feedback.

Victoria
North Cascades
National Park
11
ria
North Cascades
National Park

Mapping Out Where You Want to Be

In This Chapter

▶ Deciding what to use for navigation

▶ Using what's already on your phone

▶ Using maps safely

*H*aving a map on your phone is very handy. At the most basic level, you can ask your phone to show you a map for where you plan to go. This is convenient, but only a small part of what's possible.

With the right applications, your HTC One can do the following:

✔ Automatically find your location on a map.

✔ Give driving, walking, or public transportation directions to where you want to go.

✔ Give 2D or 2D turn-by-turn directions as you travel.

✔ Tell others where you are.

✔ Use the screen on your phone as a viewfinder to identify landmarks as you pan the area (augmented reality).

Mapping apps are useful, but they also use more battery life and data than many other applications. Be aware of the impact on your data usage and battery life. Leaving mapping applications active is convenient, but it can also be a drain on your battery and your wallet if you don't pay attention to your usage and have the wrong service plan.

Figuring Out GPS 101: First Things First

You can't talk smartphone mapping without GPS in the background, which creates a few inherent challenges. First off (and obviously), your phone has a GPS receiver. That means the following:

- ✔ **Gimme a sec.** Like all GPS receivers, your location-detection system takes a little time to determine your location when you first turn on your phone.

- ✔ **Outdoors is better.** Many common places where you use your phone — primarily, within buildings — have poor GPS coverage.

- ✔ **Nothing is perfect.** Even with good GPS coverage, location and mapping aren't perfected yet. *Augmented reality,* the option that identifies local landmarks on the screen, is even less perfect.

- ✔ **Turn me on.** Your GPS receiver must be turned on for it to work. Sure, turning it off saves battery life, but doing so precludes mapping applications from working.

- ✔ **Keep it on the down-low.** Sharing sensitive location information is of grave concern to privacy advocates. The fear is that a stalker or other villain can access your location information in your phone to track your movements. In practice, there are easier ways to accomplish this goal, but controlling who knows your location is still something you should consider, particularly when you have applications that share your location information.

Good cellular coverage has nothing to do with GPS coverage. The GPS receiver in your phone is looking for satellites; cellular coverage is based upon antennas mounted on towers or tall buildings.

Practically Speaking: Using Maps

The easiest to understand presents a local map when you open the application. Depending on the carrier on which you run, you may have mapping applications preloaded, such as Google Maps, TeleNav, or VZ Navigator. You can find them on your Home screen and in your Application list.

It's not a large leap for a smartphone to offer directions from your GPS-derived location to somewhere nearby. These are standard capabilities.

This section describes Google Maps and Google Maps Navigation; these are both free and might come preinstalled on your phone. Other mapping applications that might come with your phone, such as Bing Maps or TeleNav, have similar capabilities, but the details will be a bit different. Or you might want to use other mapping applications. That's all fine.

In addition to the general-purpose mapping applications that come on your phone, hundreds of mapping applications can help you find a favorite store, navigate waterways, or find your car in a crowded parking lot. For example, Navigon and TCS offer solutions based on real-time traffic conditions and give you-turn-by-turn directions using three-dimensional images of the neighborhoods in which you are driving. For more, see the section, "Upgrading Your Navigation," at the end of this chapter.

As nice as mapping devices are, they're too slow to tell you to stop looking at them and avoid an oncoming car. If you can't control yourself in the car and need to watch the arrow on the map screen move, do yourself a favor and let someone else drive. If no one else is available to drive, be safe and don't use the navigation service on your phone in the car.

The most basic way to use a map is to bring up the Google Maps application. Tap the icon and you'll see a street map with your location. Figure 11-1 shows an example of a map whose user is in Seattle. You'll see a blue arrow head at the center of the map. The map in Figure 11-1 starts at about one mile square. You can see other parts of the map by putting your finger on the map and dragging away from the part that you want to see.

Turn the phone to change how the map is displayed. Depending on what you're looking for, a different orientation might be easier.

Changing map scale

A resolution of one square mile will usually help you get oriented in an unfamiliar place. But sometimes it helps to zoom out to get a broader perspective, or zoom in to find familiar landmarks, like a body of water or a major highway.

To get more real estate onto the screen, use the pinch motion discussed in Chapter 2. This shrinks the size of the map and brings in more of the map around where you're pinching. Keep pinching to get more map. After you have your bearings, you can return to the original resolution by double-tapping the screen.

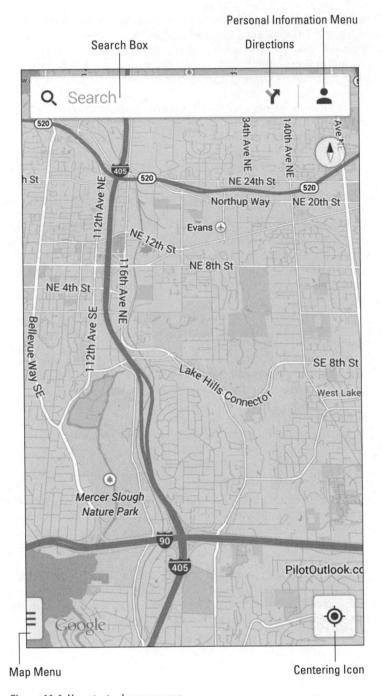

Figure 11-1: You start where you are.

On the other hand, a scale of one square mile might not be enough. To see more landmarks, use the stretch motion to zoom in. The stretch motion expands the boundaries. Continue stretching until you get the detail that you want. Figure 11-2 shows a street map both zoomed in and zoomed out. The map on the left is in Satellite View. The map on the right is zoomed out in Terrain View.

Zoomed In Image

Panned Out Image

Figure 11-2: A street image zoomed in and zoomed out.

Choose Satellite or Terrain View by tapping the menu button (pointed out in Figure 11-1) in the bottom-left corner of the map. This brings up the menu seen in Figure 11-3. You can also bring up other views that are useful to you, including transit routes and bicycling paths. I show you some of the other options later in this chapter.

If you're zooming in and can't find where you are on the map, tap the dot-surrounded-by-a-circle icon (called the *centering icon* in Figure 11-1). It moves the map so that you're in the center.

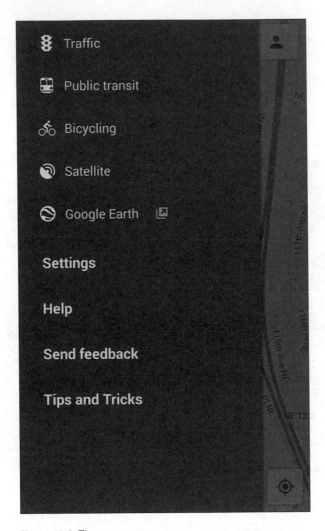

Figure 11-3: The map menu.

Finding nearby services

Most searches for services fall into a relatively few categories. Your map application is set up to find what you're most likely to seek.

1. **Tap the search icon (the magnifying glass in Figure 11-1).**

    You're offered a quick way to find the services near you: restaurants, coffee shops, bars, hotels, attractions, ATMs, and gas stations, as shown in Figure 11-4.

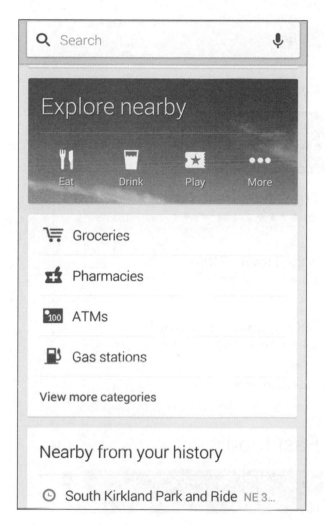

Figure 11-4: Tap to find a service on the map.

2. Tap one of the icons.

Your phone searches businesses in your immediate area. The results come back as a regular Google search with names, addresses, and distances from your location. An example is shown in Figure 11-5.

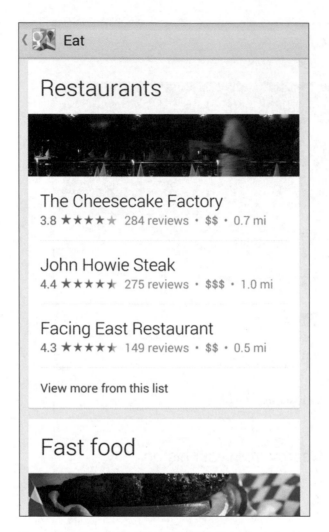

Figure 11-5: The results of a service selection.

3. **Tap an option to see more details on that business.**

   See the result in Figure 11-6.

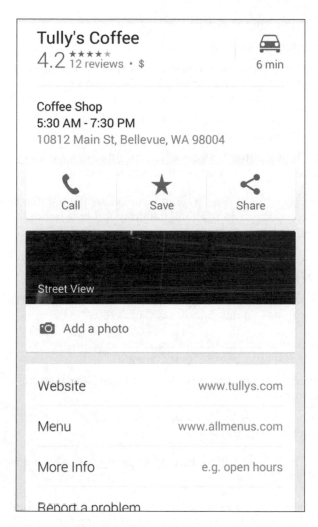

Figure 11-6: The detailed results of a service selection.

In addition to location and reviews, you'll see three icons and other relevant information:

- **Map:** Tap to see a map of where you are in relation to this business.
- **Directions:** Tap to get turn-by-turn directions from your location to this business.

You might need to download Google Maps Navigation to your phone to get the turn-by-turn directions. You can get this free app from the Play Store. For more on how to download applications, read Chapter 8.

✔ **Call:** Tap this to call the business.

✔ More options, which include

- *Street View:* See a location in Google Street View. As shown at the bottom of Figure 11-6, Street View shows a photo of the street address for the location you entered.

- *Reviews:* This includes all kinds of information about how people have experienced this location.

- *More:* Run another Google search on this business (so you can see reviews from other parts of the web, for example).

Just how deeply you dive in is up to you. In any case, having this kind of information when you're visiting an unfamiliar location is handy.

Getting and Using Directions

You probably want to get directions from your map application. I know I do. You can get directions in a number of ways, including

✔ Tap the Search text box and type the name or address of your desired location: for example, **Seattle Space Needle**.

✔ Tap the directions icon and type **Seattle Space Needle** in the Choose Destination line.

✔ Tap the services icons (refer to Figure 11-1), tap the attractions icon (refer to Figure 11-4), and select your location.

Any of these methods lead you to the map showing your desired location, as shown in Figure 11-7.

✔ **Narrow down your options** by tapping the selection you want. It might seem intuitive to get results only for the attraction you search for (such as the Seattle Space Needle). Such a result, however, is sometimes too simple. Google Map might give you several choices.

✔ **To get directions,** tap the icon with the blue silhouette of a car. If you want directions for walking, bicycling, or public transportation instead of driving, tap the menu bar and click the mode of transportation you want to use. This brings up the screen which shows the driving directions from, in this case the Bellevue City Park to the Space Needle.

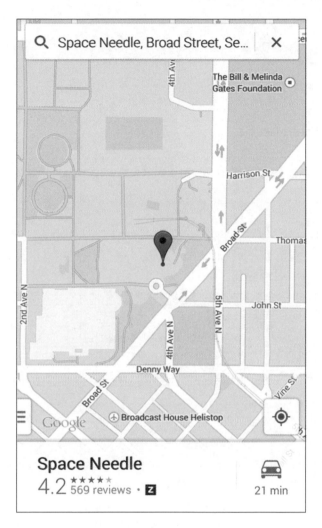

Figure 11-7: A street map search result.

✔ **To get step-by-step directions,** tap the link that says Start Navigation. This option shows where you are as you travel and tells you what to do until you arrive at our destination. See Figure 11-8.

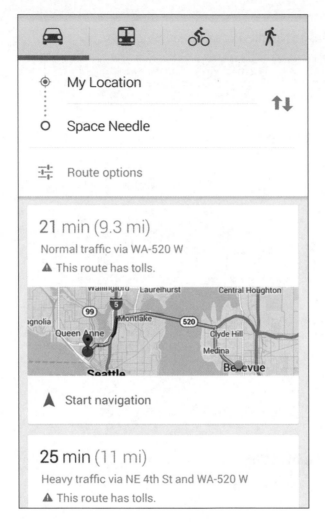

Figure 11-8: Your direction options, from original location to the target.

Upgrading Your Navigation

As a rule, free navigation applications like Google Maps Navigation use historical averages to determine travel times. The applications that charge a modest monthly fee (between $5 and $10 monthly), like VZ Navigator, have real-time updates that help you avoid congested routes. They also tend to have 3D images, like those in Figure 11-9, that provide better context for landmarks.

2D Navigation   3D Navigation

Figure 11-9: Comparing 2D navigation to 3D navigation.

The 2D map is perfectly usable and accurate, but the 3D map gives you context and additional information about the buildings around you, which can give you an extra level of confidence. So if you frequently depend on your mapping app to get where you're going, you may find a paid app worth your while.

Paying an extra $5 to $10 monthly feels like a lot for some of us. Keep in mind, however, that

- ✓ This is relatively modest compared to what you're paying monthly for your service.
- ✓ The price of a dedicated GPS receiver, with almost exactly the same capabilities, is between $125 and $200. The monthly cost of the service is comparable to the one-time fee of the GPS receiver. Plus, you don't have the hassle of lugging an additional device and its wiring.

Playing Music and Videos

In This Chapter

▶ Enjoying a single song, podcasts, or an entire album

▶ Viewing videos

▶ Knowing your licensing options

Most smartphones have built-in digital music players. Having a single device that you can use as a phone *and* as a source of music is quite convenient. You can play digital music files and podcasts all day and all night on your phone.

In addition, by virtue of the HD screen on your HTC One, your phone makes for an excellent handheld video player. Just listen on the headset and watch on the screen, whether you have a short music video or a full-length movie.

To boot, your HTC One comes with applications for downloading and listening to music as well as downloading and watching videos. These apps are very straightforward, especially if you've ever used a CD or a DVD player. In a sense, they're even easier than using a VCR — no need to set the clock!

Being Mindful of Carrier Quirks

The only possible pitfall for playing music and videos is that each carrier has its own spin: Some cellular carriers want you to use their music stores; some give you flexibility. You can use the basic multimedia tools that come with the phone, or download options that you have via the Play Store. (Read all about the Play Store in Chapter 8.)

To keep things straight, read on to see the options you have regardless of what cellular carrier you use — including basic multimedia applications that came with your phone. Lots and lots of options exist. The truth is that there isn't that much difference among them. The differences lie in price and selection.

Therefore, I cover the basic functions, but I encourage you to find the entertainment that you prefer. Trust me — it's out there somewhere. A good mainstream option is the Google Play Store, which I introduce you to in Chapter 8. However, don't worry about loyalty to this service. Find the music you like and subscribe to as many services as it takes to bring you joy.

Remember, the whole point is enjoyment. Enjoy yourself!

Are You Not Entertained?

Regardless of whether you have an M8, what app you use for entertainment, and whether you're listening to audio or watching video, here's where I cover some common considerations.

✔ You use *headphones* with your MP3 player, but your phone uses a *headset*. The vocabulary is more than just semantics; a headset has headphones plus a microphone so you can make and take phone calls.

✔ You need to know about connecting your HTC One to a television or stereo. After I talk about that, I cover the issue of licensing multimedia material.

Choosing your headset options

You can use wired or wireless (Bluetooth) headsets with your HTC One. Wired headsets are generally less expensive than Bluetooth headsets of similar quality, and of course, wired headsets don't need charging, as do the Bluetooth headsets.

On the other hand, you lose freedom of mobility if you're tangled up in wires. In addition, the battery in Bluetooth headsets last much longer than the battery in your phone.

Wired headsets

At the bottom of your HTC One is a headset jack. If you try to use your regular headphone jack in this jack, you'll hear the audio, but the person on the other end of the call may not hear you because the headphones don't come with a microphone. In such a case, your phone tries to use the built-in mic as a speakerphone. Depending upon the ambient noise conditions, it may work fine or sound awful. Of course, you can always ask the person you're talking to whether he can hear you.

To address that problem, your phone might come with a wired headset. In that case, just plug it in to use the device. The HTC One uses ear buds, like those shown in Figure 12-1.

Figure 12-1: A typical wired headset with ear buds and a 3.5mm plug.

Some people dislike ear buds. You can get other styles at stores that offer the following options, including

- ✔ Around-the-ear headphones that place the speakers on the ear and are held in place with a clip
- ✔ A behind-the-neck band that holds around-the-ear headphones in place
- ✔ An over-the-head band that places the headphones on the ear

The laws in some regions prohibit the use of headphones while driving. Correcting the officer and explaining that these are really "headsets" and not "headphones" won't help your case if you're pulled over. Even if not explicitly illegal in an area, it's still a bad idea to play music in both ears at a volume that inhibits your ability to hear warnings while driving.

Ear buds can have a greater chance of causing ear damage if the volume is too loud than other options. The close proximity to your ear drum is the culprit. There are probably warnings on the ear bud instructions, but I wanted to amplify this information (*har har*).

In any case, give yourself some time to get used to any new headset. There is often an adjustment period while you get used to having a foreign object in or around your ear.

Stereo Bluetooth headsets

The other option is to use a stereo Bluetooth headset. Figure 12-2 shows a typical model. A stereo Bluetooth headset is paired the same way as any other Bluetooth headset. (Read how to do this in Chapter 3.) When your HTC One and the headset connect, the phone recognizes that the headset operates in stereo when you're listening to music or videos.

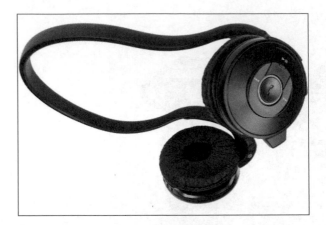

Figure 12-2: A behind-the-neck Bluetooth stereo headset.

There are also several variations on how to place the headphone part of the headset near your ear with a Bluetooth headset. Be aware that some products on the market are strictly Bluetooth head*phones*, and not headsets; they don't have microphones. In this case, you might want to remove your headphones when a call comes in, or move the phone near your mouth. Of course, this effort defeats some of the convenience of having a Bluetooth connection.

Choosing your Bluetooth speaker options

In the last two years, developers released a flurry of products known as *Bluetooth speakers*. Among the better-known Bluetooth speakers are products such as the Dre Beats Pill. These speakers include a range of options, some of which are very small and convenient; others are designed to offer excellent audio quality.

Although these speakers (which come in a range of sizes) are not as portable as the Bluetooth headset — they're a little difficult to use as you're walking down the street — they're usually pretty easy to take with you and set up when you're at a desk or in someone's living room. They also do not need a cable to make a connection, and are always ready to go.

Soen Audio's Transit (see Figure 12-3) is an excellent example of a high-quality Bluetooth speaker. Its list price is close to $200. If you like high-quality sound, this is the quality of Bluetooth speaker that you'd want to get. On the other hand, if you're just looking for background enjoyment, you can get a Bluetooth speaker for less than half that price.

Figure 12-3: The Soen Audio's Transit speaker.

Connecting to your stereo or TV

You can connect your HTC One to your stereo. You can also connect your phone to your TV. There are distinct approaches to connection if you're connecting just audio to your stereo or audio and video to your TV.

Connecting to your stereo

Although being able to listen to your music on the move is convenient, it's also nice to listen on your home or car stereo. Your HTC One presents your stereo with a nearly perfect version of what went in. The sound quality that comes out is limited only by the quality of your stereo.

In addition, you can play the music files and playlists stored on your phone, which can be more convenient than playing CDs. Setup involves

1. **Plug the 3.5mm jack from the cable in Figure 12-4 into the 3.5mm jack available on newer stereos.**

2. **Choose the AUX setting.**

3. **Be entertained.**

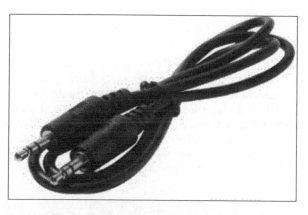

Figure 12-4: The patch cable with 3.5mm plugs.

Connecting to your HD TV

You can also play videos from your phone on your TV — but you need a few things:

- ✔ **An HTC HDTV Media Link.** The list price is about $85, but you can find this on sale on the Internet for a few dollars less.

- ✔ **A standard HDMI cable.** If you have an HDTV, this is a standard cable. If you don't have one handy, you can borrow one from your game console. I'm sure your kids won't mind as long as you put things back the way you found them when you're done.

- ✔ **Your USB cable/charger** (that you use to charge your phone). Connecting your phone to an HDTV draws a lot of power. Charging your phone while you watch TV is a good way to ensure you don't miss an important call.

Licensing your multimedia files

It's really quite simple: You need to pay the artist if you're going to listen to music or watch video with integrity. Many low-cost options are suitable for any budget. Depending upon how much you plan to listen to music and podcasts or watch videos, you can figure out what's the best deal.

You can buy or lease music, podcasts, or videos. In most cases, you pay for them with a credit card. And depending upon your cellular carrier, you might be allowed to pay for them on your monthly cellular bill.

Stealing music or videos is uncool. Although it might be technically possible to play pirated music and videos on your phone, it's stealing. Don't do it.

Listening up on licensing

Three primary licensing options are available for music files and podcasts:

- ✔ **By the track:** Pay for each song individually. A typical song costs about 79 to 99 cents. Podcasts, which are frequently used for radio shows, speeches, or lectures, can vary dramatically in price.

- ✔ **By the album:** Buying an album isn't a holdover from the days before digital music. Music artists and producers create albums with an organization of songs that offer a consistent feeling or mood. Although many music-playing applications allow you to assemble your own playlist, an album is created by professionals. In addition, buying a full album is often less expensive than on a per-song basis. You can get multiple songs for $8 to $12. See Figure 12-5 to see some albums in My Library.

- ✔ **With a monthly pass:** The last option for buying audio files is the monthly pass. For about $15 per month, you can download as much music as you want from the service provider's library.

If you let your subscription to your monthly pass provider lapse, you won't be able to listen to the music from this library.

In addition to full access to the music library, some music library providers offer special services to introduce you to music that's similar to what you've been playing. These services are a very convenient way to learn about new music. If you have even a small interest in expanding your music repertoire, these services are an easy way to do it.

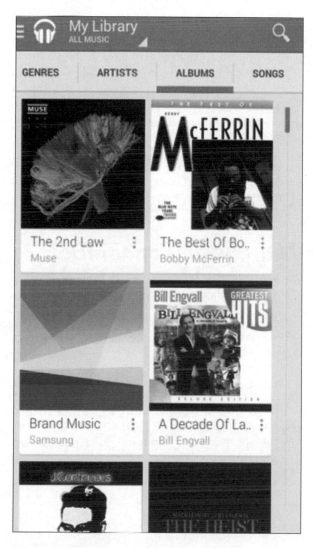

Figure 12-5: My Library can show by genre, artist, album, and song.

Whether buying or renting is most economical depends on your listening and viewing habits. If you don't plan to buy much, or you know specifically what you want, you may save some money by paying for all your files individually. If you're not really sure what you want, or you like a huge variety of things, paying for monthly access might make better sense.

Licensing for videos

The two primary licensing options available for videos are

- ✔ **Rental:** This option is similar to renting a video from a store. You can watch the video as many times as you like within 24 hours from the start of the first play. In addition, the first play must begin within a defined period, such as a week, of your downloading it. Most movies are in the $3 to $5 range.

- ✔ **Purchase:** You have a license to watch the file as frequently as you want, for as long as you want. The purchase cost can be as low as $12, but is more typically in the $15 range.

At the moment, no sources for mainstream Hollywood films allow you to buy a monthly subscription and give you unlimited access to a film library. This can change at any time, so watch for announcements.

Enjoying Basic Multimedia Capabilities

Regardless of the carrier for your HTC One, some basic multimedia capabilities are common across the different phones.

Your phone comes with the Music Player and Video Player applications, and you might have other multimedia applications as well, depending upon your carrier.

Don't worry about storage capacity for your music. A very rough estimate is that a gigabyte (GB) of storage will store 120 hours of music. The memory cards that come with your phone can store up to 32GB. You can also buy memory cards these days that can store 128GB at a cost of about $150. There are limits on storing videos, however. About one full-length movie takes up 1GB. Don't bother trying to put your entire video collection on your phone unless you have a small collection.

Grooving with the Music Player app

The Music Player app allows you to play music and audio files. The first step is to get music and audio files for your phone.

Some ways to acquire music and/or recordings for your phone are

- ✔ Buy and download tracks from an online music store.
- ✔ Load them on your MicroSD memory card from the digital music collection on your PC.
- ✔ Receive them as attachments via email or text message.
- ✔ Receive them from another device connected with a Bluetooth link.
- ✔ Record them on your phone.

Buying from an online music store

The most straightforward method of getting music on your phone is from an online music store. You can download a wide variety of music from dozens of mainstream online music stores. The Play Store is an option. In addition to apps, it has music and video. Other well-known sites include Rhapsody, Amazon MP3, VEVO, and last.fm. In addition, many more specialty or "boutique" stores provide things you can't get from the mass-market stores. For example, MAQAM offers Middle Eastern music (www.maqammp3.com).

The steps you take to buy music from online stores vary from store to store. Ultimately, there are more similarities than differences. As an example of when you know what you want — what you really, really want — here's how to find and download the song "Wannabe" by the Spice Girls. I'm using Amazon MP3. If you don't have Amazon MP3 in your application list, you would start by loading that app on your phone, as I describe in Chapter 8. When you open it, you see the screen shown in Figure 12-6.

From here, you can search for music by album, song, or music genre. Amazon MP3 offers a different free music track and an album at a deep discount every day.

To pay for files at an online music store, you need an account and a credit card. This process is similar, if not identical, to signing up for Play Store; see Chapter 8. You need your email account, a password, and in some cases, an account name. In the case of Amazon MP3, you already have an account if you have an account with Amazon. If not, you're asked to create an account.

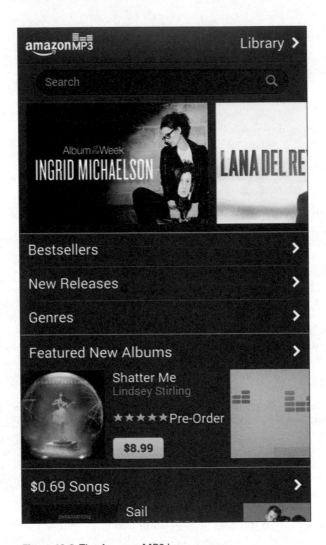

Figure 12-6: The Amazon MP3 home screen.

Now search for the song you want:

1. **Enter the relevant information in the Amazon MP3 Search field.**

   In this case, I'm searching for "Wannabe" by the Spice Girls. The search result can come up with all kinds of options, including albums, individual tracks, similar songs, and other songs from the same artist. Be ready for these options.

2. **To buy the track, tap twice on the price.**

   The left screen in Figure 12-7 shows the price. When you tap once on the price, you get a confirmation message to make sure that you want to buy the download; the price is replaced with a Buy icon, as shown on the right in Figure 12-7. To buy, tap Buy.

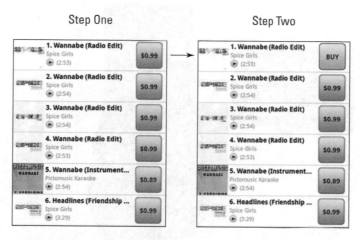

Figure 12-7: Tap twice to buy.

3. **Sign in with your account information.**

   Unless you're going to subsist on the free MP3 files you can get from this site, you need to pay. After you enter this information, the file automatically starts downloading to your phone. A progress screen lets you know when you're finished. The song is now loaded on your phone. When you open the music player, it's ready for you to play.

Loading digital music from your PC

In addition to acquiring music files from an online music store, you can transfer digital music tracks stored on your PC. The challenge is choosing the method for transferring files from your PC to your phone.

✔ If you plan to download one or a few files, using email is most convenient. The next section covers receiving music files as email attachments.

✔ If you plan to move a large music library from your PC to your phone, load the memory card from your phone by connecting it to your PC.

You'll need to use an *adapter* — a card reader — that allows you to insert your MicroSD memory in a holder with a standard USB connection. Figure 12-8 shows one such adapter in use with the memory card. The actual size of the card is about as big as the fingernail on your pinky.

Figure 12-8: A MicroSD card and a USB adapter.

Your HTC One may or may not come with a MicroSD card. Even if it does come with one, you can buy cards with larger capacity if you wish. Prices for these memory cards have been dropping, but as a ballpark, an 8GB card will run you $5, and you'll pay about $20 for 32GB and $40 for 64GB. Expect to pay more at a cellular carrier's retail store, however.

If you've ever used a thumb drive to transfer a file from one PC to another, you'll find the process similar when you're copying music files to your phone via the MicroSD card:

1. **Turn off your phone.**

2. **Remove the MicroSD card tray as described in Chapter 2.**

3. **Remove the MicroSD card from your phone.**

   The memory card lies flat in its slot. To remove it, use the removal tool and then your fingernail to pull it out of its slot.

4. **Insert your memory card into your adapter.**

5. **Plug your adapter into your PC.**

   When you plug the USB MicroSD Adapter into a USB port, your PC recognizes it as just another *thumb drive* (a removable disk) and asks what you want to do.

6. **Click Open Folder to View Files.**

   This opens a window with the files on your MicroSD card.

7. **On your PC, open the folder that has your digital music and copy the files you want to your MicroSD card.**

   Don't worry about which folder to use to place the files. Your phone is happy to do that for you.

8. **After all the files are copied, eject the adapter MicroSD card from your PC.**

9. **Remove the MicroSD card from your adapter and put it back in your phone.**

10. **Turn on your phone.**

    Your phone sees these new files, knows that they are audio files, and organizes them for you when you open up the Music Player app. Done.

Receiving music as an attachment

As long as you comply with your license agreement, you can email or text a music file as an attachment to anyone, including yourself.

1. **Simply send yourself an email from your PC with the desired music file.**

2. **Open the email or text on your phone, as shown in Figure 12-9.**

3. **Tap Save.**

   The file is saved on your phone and accessible from the Music Player app. Done.

Your phone can play music files that come in any of the following formats: FLAC, WAV, Vorbis, MP3, AAC, AAC+, eAAC+, WMA, AMR-NB, AMR-WB, MID, AC3, and XMF.

Recording sounds on your phone

No one else thinks your kids' rendition of "Happy Birthday" is anything special, but you treasure it. In fact, your phone probably comes with a recording app.

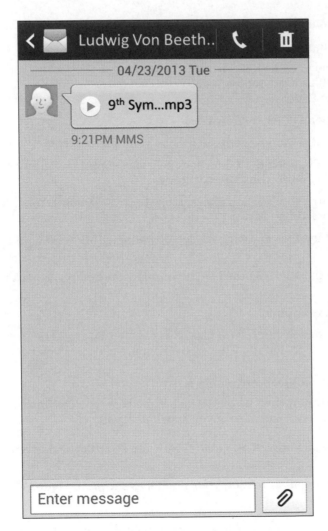

Figure 12-9: A text with an attached music file.

In general, a simple record button creates a sound file when you finish recording. If one did not come with your phone, dozens upon dozens of voice recorders are free for download at the Play Store. The sound quality might not be the best, but what you record can be just as important or entertaining as what you buy commercially. Your phone treats all audio files the same and all are playable on your Music Player.

Playing downloaded music

To play your music, open the Music Player application.

Just tap that icon. The first screen that you see sorts your music files into a number of categories.

The categories include

- ✔ **Playlists:** Some digital music stores bundle songs into playlists, such as Top Hits from the Fifties. You can also create your own playlists (such as songs from your twenties when you're in your fifties).
- ✔ **Recent:** This list is for the songs you most recently added to you collection.
- ✔ **Artists:** This category lists all songs from all the albums from a given artist.
- ✔ **Albums:** Tapping this category places all your songs into an album with which the song is associated. When you tap the album, you see all the songs you've purchased, whether one song or all the songs from that album.
- ✔ **Songs:** This lists all your song files in alphabetic order.
- ✔ **Genres:** This category separates music into genres, such as country and western or heavy metal.

These categories are useful when you have a large number of files. To play a song, album, or genre, open that category and tap the song, playlist, album, artist, or genre. The song will start playing.

Adding songs as ringtones and alarms

Here's how to add a song as a ringtone or alarm:

1. **Open a contact.**

   A generic contact is seen in Figure 12-10. Refer to Chapter 6 if you have any questions about contacts or the People application.

2. **Tap the Ringtone link.**

   The edit page opens for the contact. A quick scan finds that "Ode to Joy" is not among the options that come with your phone. To use a music file as a ringtone, find the plus sign at the top of page.

3. **Tap the plus sign.**

   The music files on your phone are listed.

4. **Highlight the song you want and tap OK.**

   From now on, when you hear this song, you know it will be your friend Ludwig when "Ode to Joy" starts playing on your phone.

Creating playlists

Next to each song or album is a gray arrowhead pointing down and to the right. Tap the menu option icon (three vertical dots) for options. You can add a song to a playlist. See Figure 12-11.

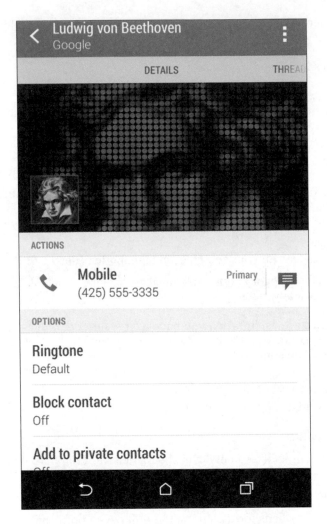

Figure 12-10: A typical contact for a Baroque composer.

Jamming to Internet radio

If you have not tried Internet radio, you should definitely consider it. The basic idea is that you enter information on your current music favorites, and these services play music that is similar. Pandora and Slacker Radio are two of the best known; one or the other may be on your phone already. If not, they're available for download from the Play Store. Figure 12-12 shows some of the 9,000 Internet radio apps in the Play Store.

Track Menu option icon

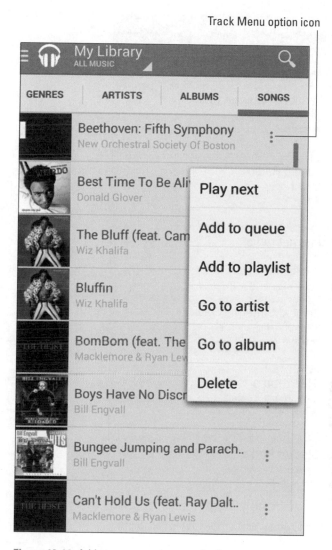

Figure 12-11: Add some songs to your playlist.

These apps are a great way to learn about new songs and groups that may appeal to you. The service streams music to your phone for you to enjoy. You can buy the track if you choose.

Streaming audio files (which is what you're doing when listening to music on your phone via Internet radio) can use a large amount of data over time. This may be no problem if you have an unlimited or large data-service plan. Otherwise your "free" Internet radio service can wind up costing you a lot. You're best off using Wi-Fi.

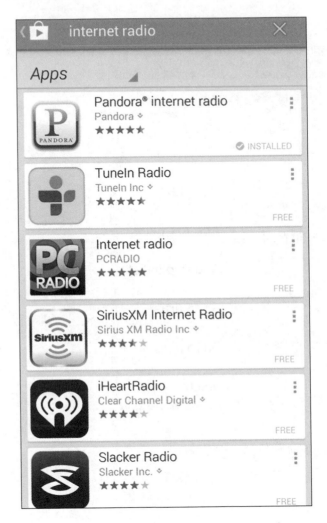

Figure 12-12: Some Internet radio options in the Play Store.

Looking at your video options

The Music Player app plays music. Similarly, you use Play Movie and TV to play videos. Play Movie and TV is in your app list and might even be on your Home screen. In most ways, playing videos is the same as playing audio with a few exceptions:

✔ Many people prefer to buy music, but renting is more typical for videos.

✔ Video files are usually, but not always, larger.

Otherwise, as with music files, you can acquire videos for your phone from an online video store — and you need to have an account and pay for the use. In addition, you can download video files to your phone, and Play Movie and TV will play them like a VCR or DVD player.

Your videos come in four categories:

- Top Selling Movies
- New Movie Releases
- Top TV Shows
- Top TV Episodes

In Chapter 9, I cover how to use the digital camcorder on your phone. You can watch any video you've shot on your phone: From the Google Play application, scroll over to the Personal Video section. To play your video, simply tap the name of the file. The app begins showing the video in landscape orientation. The controls that pop up when you tap the screen are similar to a VCR or DVD player.

Your phone can show the following video formats: MPEG-4, WMV, AVI/DivX, MKV, and FLV.

Skyping with Your HTC One

It's a good time to bring up a very popular capability: video chat. Video chatting, long predicted as the next great thing by Ma Bell since the 1960s, is finally coming on strong. The good news is that your HTC One is the ideal platform for having video chats.

This section focuses on Skype video chat, which falls into the "cool capabilities" side of the equation.

Signing in to Skype

From there, you have three scenarios for getting access to Skype:

- **Use your existing Skype account:** This is if you already have a Skype account on, say, your PC.

- **Sign in with your Microsoft account:** If you already have an email account with Microsoft, you don't need to create a separate Skype account. You can tell that you have a Microsoft account if your email address ends in @msn.com, @live.com, or @hotmail.com.

- **Create a new Skype account:** You use this option if you don't already have a Skype or Microsoft account.

Pie in the Skype

You may have heard talk about Skype. It was originally an Internet telephony application that allowed you to make calls from your PC to another PC that also had Skype. Over the years, this application has evolved in terms of technology, the platforms on which it operates, and its future.

At first, Skype was a convenient way to get around traditional telephone charges, especially for long distance. This was particularly economical when calling internationally; in fact, the application traces its roots to a team of developers from Estonia. Also, the PC was its original platform. Now it happily runs on many smartphone platforms, including Android.

Skype has traveled far from its humble beginnings. We now use bigger phrases, like *communication platform for end-users*, to describe its prospects for the future. The app has some cool capabilities, like automatically integrating hyperlinked Skype numbers into Microsoft Office documents whenever possible.

Follow these steps to get started:

1. **Enter your account number and skip to the next section.**

   If you don't already have an account, tap the Create a Skype Account link at the bottom of the page.

   Before you start entering information, you're greeted with a warning that lets you know that you can't use Skype to dial 911. There's no need to worry. Your cellular phone is there in case you need to dial 911.

2. **Tap the link that says I Agree.**

   You'll see the account-creation page shown in Figure 12-13.

   The app is pretty smart.

3. **Add +1 to your telephone number.**

   However, when you try to create an account with this number, the app will reject it. It wants the International prefix: You need to enter a +1 before you type the ten digits we use in the United States. (Hey, I said the app was pretty smart, not perfect!)

   If you like the options it chooses for you, take them. Otherwise, try your own. If the username Skype chooses is available, it's yours to use. If not, try again. After you create an account, you're taken to the Skype page (see Figure 12-14).

Creating Skype contacts

You're going to need someone to chat with. Figure 12-15 shows populated contacts.

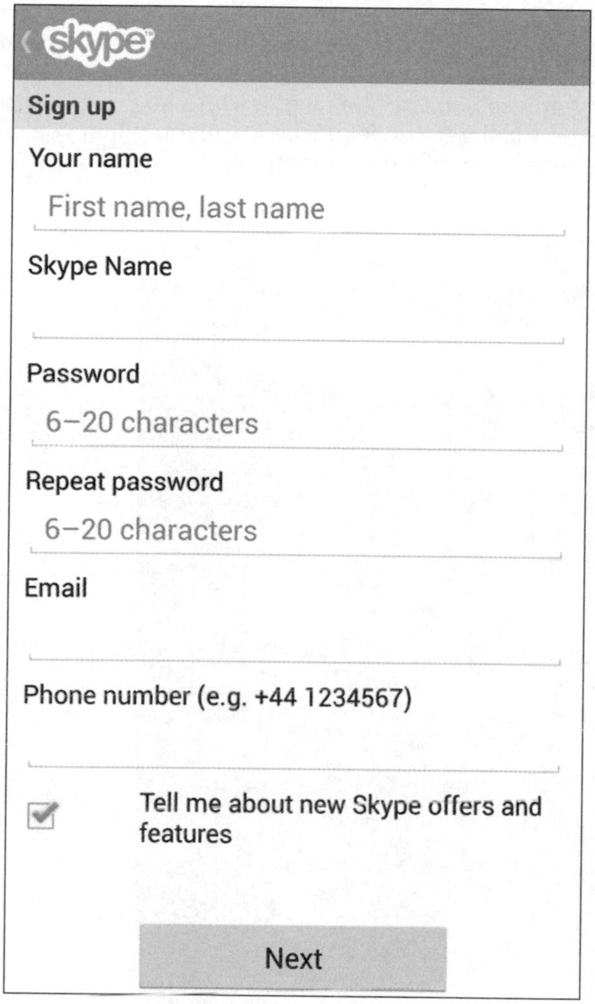

Skype

Sign up

Your name

First name, last name

Skype Name

Password

6–20 characters

Repeat password

6–20 characters

Email

Phone number (e.g. +44 1234567)

☑ Tell me about new Skype offers and features

Next

Figure 12-13: The Skype account-creation page.

1. **On the Skype Home screen, tap the Contacts icon.**

2. **Tap the menu button.**

   Three options come up.

3. **Choose an option:**

   - *Add Contacts:* Search Skype's directory for contacts who already have a Skype account.

   - *Save Number:* If you know someone with an account, you can manually add that person's number.

• *Search Address Book:* This is the easiest option. Skype compares your contacts to the database of Skype users to find all matches.

The Search Address Book option takes a while, so you may want to set up your phone on a charger and let it run overnight. When you come back, your friends will be ready to video chat with you.

Figure 12-14: Skype page.

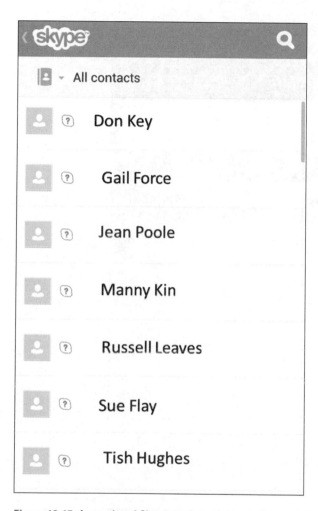

Figure 12-15: A populated Skype contacts page.

Setting up a Skype video chat

This is the easy part. If you can dial a phone, you can dial a video chat.

1. **In your Skype contacts, tap the name of the person you want to video chat with.**

   A list of connection options opens. See Figure 12-16.

2. **Tap the Video Call option.**

3. **When your friend answers, you're connected.**

   When you're connected, you see a screen remarkably reminiscent of the Skype promotional image seen Figure 12-17 (except that you and your friend are there instead of the models).

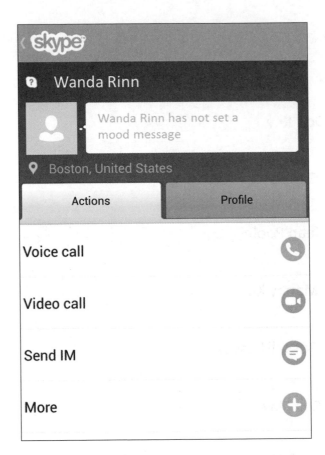

Figure 12-16: Your options.

Figure 12-17: A Skype video call.

Part V
Productivity Applications

Add a security app to your phone at www.dummies.com/extras/htconem8.

In this part . . .

- ✔ Download your calendars to your phone and upload new events to your electronic calendar.

- ✔ Use mobile Office applications from your phone or from the cloud.

- ✔ Dictate an email or text.

- ✔ Tell your phone to make a call.

Marking It on the Calendar

In This Chapter

▶ Setting up events

▶ Downloading your calendars to your phone

▶ Syncing events across calendars

ou might fall in love with your HTC One so much that you want to ask it out on a date. And speaking of dates, let's talk about your phone's calendar. The HTC One Calendar is powerful, and it can make your life easier. With just a few taps, you can bring all your electronic calendars together to keep your life synchronized.

In this chapter, I show you how to set up the calendar that comes with your phone, which might be all you need. The odds are, though, that you have calendars elsewhere, such as on your work computer. So I also show you how to combine all your calendars with your HTC One. After you read this chapter, you'll have no excuse for missing a meeting. (Or, okay, a date.)

 Some calendars use the term *appointments* for *events*. They are the same idea. I use the term *events*.

Syncing Calendars

Most likely, you already have at least two electronic calendars scattered in different places: a calendar tied to your work computer and a personal calendar. Now you have a third one — the one on your HTC phone is synced to Gmail.

Bringing together all your electronic calendars to one place, though, is one of the best things about your phone — as long as you're a faithful user of your electronic calendars, that is. To begin this process, you need to provide authorization to the respective places that your calendars are stored. This authorization is necessary to respect your privacy.

If your phone doesn't have a Calendar icon on its Home screen, open Calendar from your app list. When you first open it, you see a monthly calendar, as shown in Figure 13-1. I discuss other calendar views later in this chapter.

Change View icon   Options Menu icon

☰ Month		Today	✚	⋮

| ‹ | | **March**, 2014 | | › |

Sun	Mon	Tue	Wed	Thu	Fri	Sat
23	24	25	26	27	28	1
2	3	4	5	6	7	8
9 Daylight Saving Time st arts	10	11	12	13	14	15
16	17	18	19	20	21	22
23	24	25	26	27	28	29
30	31	1	2	3	4	5

Figure 13-1: The monthly calendar display.

The calendar on your phone might already be populated with events from your work and personal calendars. Don't be concerned — this is good news! If you've already set up your phone to *sync* (combine) with your email and your calendar (see Chapter 5), your calendars are already synchronizing with your phone.

When you add an account to your phone, such as your personal or work email account, your Facebook account, or Dropbox, you're asked whether you want to sync your calendar. The default setting for syncing is typically every hour. For most of us, this works. If you're lucky enough to have other people regularly sending you meeting invitations, however, you could get out of sync.

Follow these steps to tell your phone to sync with your calendars and get all your appointments up to the minute:

1. **From anywhere in the Calendar app (including the one shown in Figure 13-1), tap the menu icon.**

   A menu appears, as shown in Figure 13-2.

2. **Tap Sync.**

3. **Wait a few moments for the system to sync.**

   All the calendars synced to your phone are listed under the Manage Accounts section. Syncing shouldn't take long, but it does take some time. Unless you get a warning message that alerts you to a communications problem, your phone now has the latest information on appointments and meeting requests. Your phone continues to sync automatically, regardless of how often you ask it to sync manually. It does all this syncing in the background; you may not even notice that changes are going on.

You could encounter scheduling conflicts if others can create events for you on your digital calendar. Be aware of this possibility. It can be annoying (or worse) to think you have free time, offer it to someone, and then find that someone else booked you. You can avoid this problem by syncing your calendar manually before you tell someone that you have a time slot free. I explain how to do this later in this chapter.

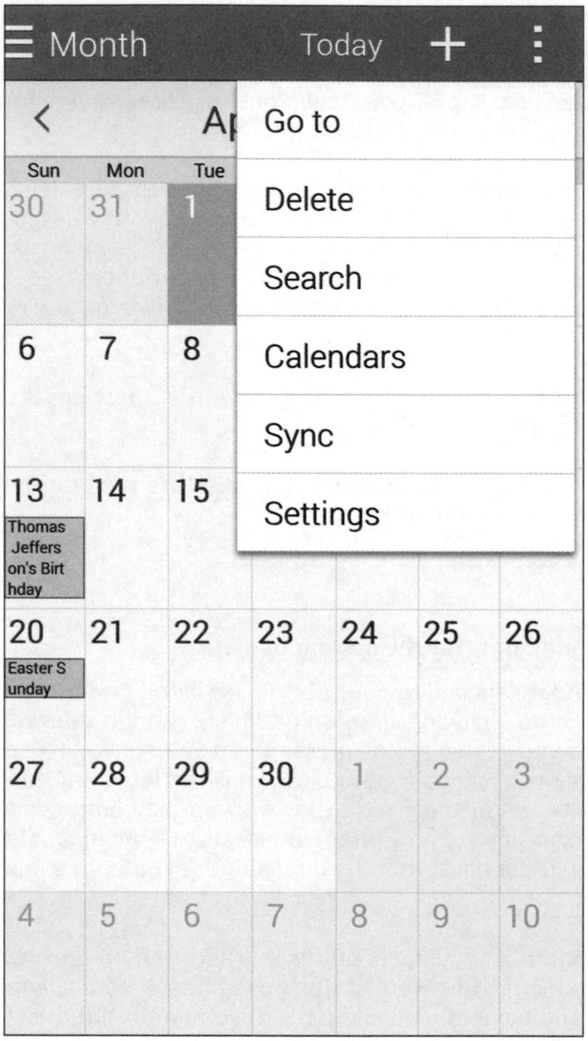

| ☰ Month | | Today | + | ⋮ |

<		Aₚ	Go to		
Sun	Mon	Tue			
30	31	1	Delete		
			Search		
6	7	8	Calendars		
			Sync		
13	14	15	Settings		
Thomas Jeffers on's Birt hday					
20	21	22	23	24	25	26
Easter S unday						
27	28	29	30	1	2	3
4	5	6	7	8	9	10

Figure 13-2: This menu pops up when you tap the three dots.

Getting in Sync with How Often You Sync

It doesn't take much battery power to sync, but the drain does add up over time. One option to save some battery life is to reduce the sync frequency. On the other hand, you may find that the lags between updates to your calendar are too long, and the syncing isn't frequent enough.

The way to adjust how frequently your phone syncs depends on the kind of account that's providing the calendar. The good news is that all these accounts are stored in one place: the Accounts tab. Tap the Settings tab to see all the email accounts (see Chapter 5) and some apps that you added (see Chapter 8). To reset the sync frequency, tap the account and pick the option you need.

Setting Calendar Display Preferences

Before you get too far into playing around with your calendar, you'll want to choose how you view it.

If you don't have a lot of events, using the month calendar shown in Figure 13-1 is probably a fine option. On the other hand, if your day is jam-packed with personal and professional events, the daily or weekly schedules might prove more practical. Switching views is easy.

1. **Tap the change view icon pointed out back in Figure 13-1.**

   The options shown in Figure 13-3 appear.

2. **Choose an option: Year, Month, Month and Agenda, Week, Day, or Agenda.**

   The time-based calendars typically display events as blocked-out times on your calendar. An alternative view is to show the events in order, like you see in Figure 13-4 for the Agenda option. With it you can see which days you have something going; the next items are at the bottom of the screen.

This shows events you have upcoming, regardless of the day they're on. This is useful for people who tend to work on events until they are done rather than on a set time. Also, this approach may make it easier for someone to get her head around what is coming her way.

Month and Agenda is a hybrid. You can see in Figure 13-5 that the calendar shows which days you have something going on and then lists the next items at the bottom of the screen.

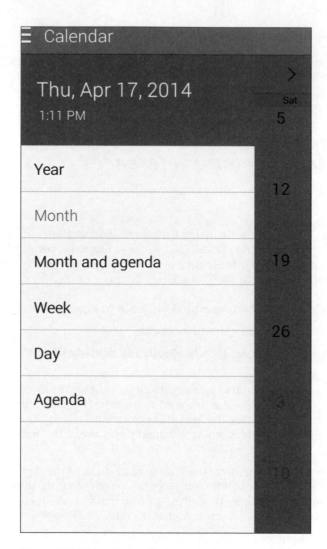

Figure 13-3: The calendar display options.

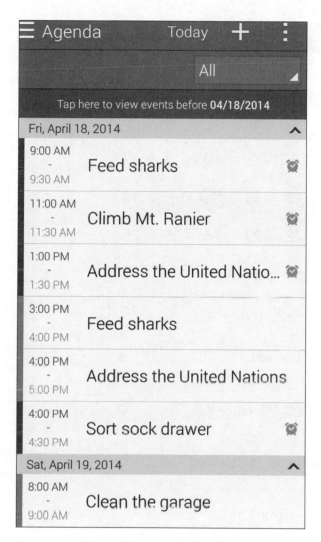

Figure 13-4: The Calendar's Agenda display.

Setting Other Display Options

You can set personal preferences for your calendar. To get to the settings for the calendar, tap the menu icon (at the top right of the screen in Figure 13-1) and tap Settings. Doing so brings up the screen shown in Figure 13-6.

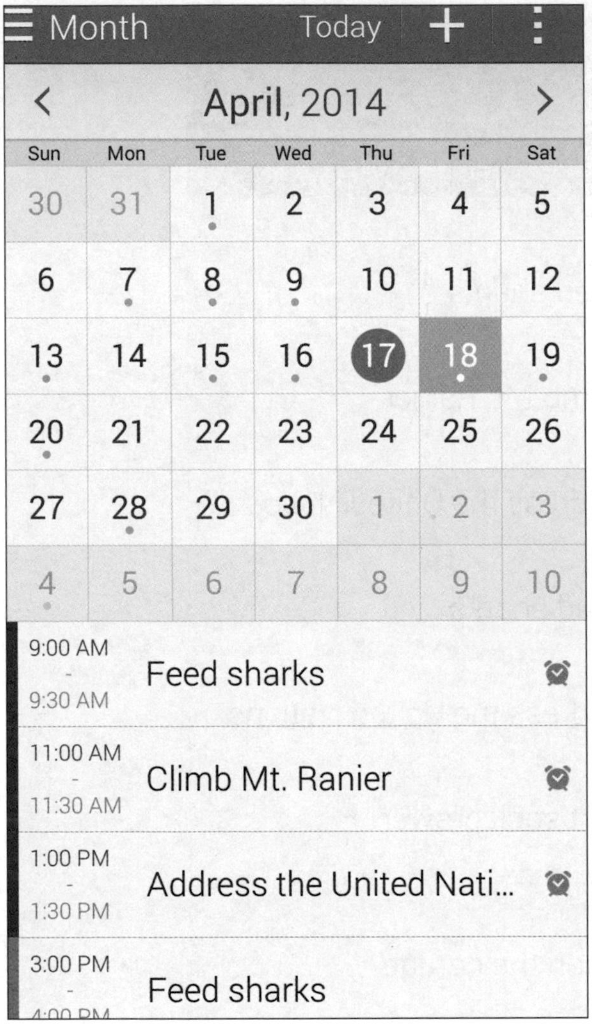

Figure 13-5: Month and Agenda combines views.

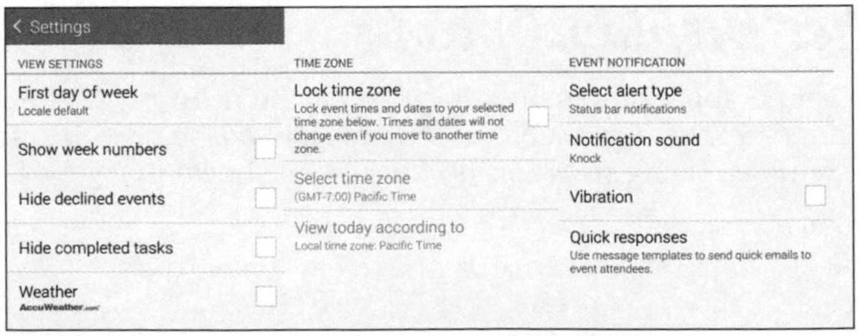

Figure 13-6: The Settings options for the Calendar application.

You have the following options:

- ✓ **First Day of Week:** The standard in the United States is that a week is displayed from Sunday to Saturday. If you prefer the week to start on Saturday or Monday, you can change it here.

- ✓ **Show Week Number:** Some people prefer to see the week number on the weekly calendar. If you count yourself among those, check this option.

- ✓ **Hide Declined Events:** When some of us decline an event, we don't care to hear about it again. Others may want to keep a reminder of the declined event in case the situation changes (or in case nothing better comes along). The default setting is to hide declined events; if you want to see them, deselect this box.

- ✓ **Hide Completed Tasks:** Some people use their calendar to track tasks in addition to appointments. Like the previous option, you can view these or hide them.

- ✓ **Weather:** You have the option of showing the weather forecast on your calendar. You want to give it a try, click this option.

- ✓ **Lock Time Zone:** When you travel to a new time zone, your phone automatically takes on the new time zone. Under most circumstances, this is a nice convenience. However, it may be confusing to some. If you prefer that the calendar remain in your home time zone, check this option. If you *do* lock the time zone, the next two options stop being grayed out and let you select your time zone and viewing options.

- ✓ **Set Alert type:** When an event is approaching, you can have the phone alert you with a pop-up, signal a notification on the status line, or do nothing. The default is to give you a notification, but you can change that option here.

- ✓ **Select Notification sound:** If you get notifications for events, you can use the Select Notification sound option to get an aural announcement that the time has arrived.

- ✓ **Vibration:** Similarly, if you enable the option that notifies you of events, you can have the phone vibrate at the proper time.

- ✓ **Quick Reponses:** This option is cool. If you get a notification, but something has come up and you can't attend, you can send a message to the meeting organizer. There are some prepared responses you can send or you create your own.

Creating an Event on the Right Calendar

You're going to create an event. It's practically a smartphone's reason for being. It's even more important to make sure that the event ends up on the right calendar. This section covers the steps to make this happen.

Creating, editing, and deleting an event

You can create an event by tapping the calendar itself twice.

Here's how to create an event — referred to as (well, yeah) an *event* — on your phone.

1. **Open the Calendar app.**

   You can create an event from different calendar displays.

2. **Tap the plus (+) sign.**

   You see the screen shown in Figure 13-7.

3. **Enter an event name.**

   Call it something descriptive so you can remember what it is without having to open it up.

4. **Choose To and From dates and start/end times.**

   Select the All Day box if the event is a full-day event.

5. **Decide which calendar you want to keep this event.**

   Figure 13-7 shows the default. When you tap this selection, the phone presents the other calendars you've synced to your phone; see Figure 13-8. You can store an event on any of them.

6. **Enter something in the Location text box.**

   Type anything that is helpful to you, such as a room number or a store name. The friendly folks at Google have built in the option to select a map location, which is accessible by tapping the Google Map icon next to the location field.

7. **(Optional) Enter more details:**

   - *Reminder:* This gives you the option to send out a notification a few minutes or a few hours before the actual event.

   - *Repeat:* This option is useful for recurring events, such as weekly meetings.

   - *Description:* This text box is handy for any notes.

   - *Time Zone:* This option helps you avoid the all-to-common mistake of setting a meeting in the wrong time zone.

8. **Tap Save.**

   The event is stored in whichever calendar you selected when you sync. If you're worried, go ahead and sync right away.

After you save an event, you can edit or delete it:

✔ **Edit:** Tap the event from a calendar view. Then tap the Pencil icon. This brings up the option to edit your event. Make your changes and tap Save. It's changed when it syncs.

▶ **Delete:** Tap the event. Tap the garbage can icon. This brings up the warning pop-up about deleting the event. Tap OK. The event is gone.

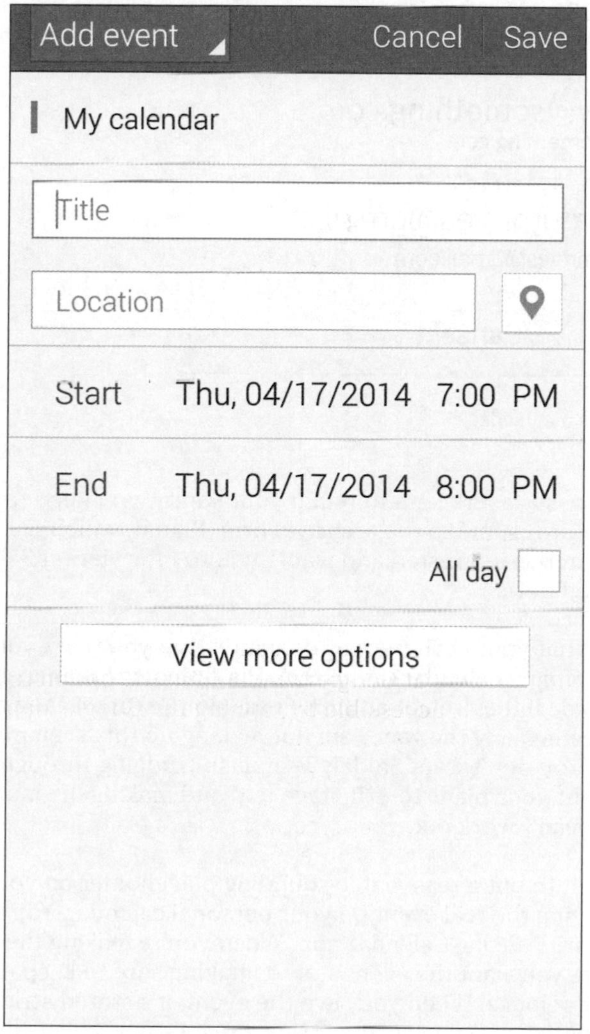

| Add event ◢ | Cancel | Save |

| My calendar |

| Title |

| Location | 📍 |

| Start | Thu, 04/17/2014 | 7:00 PM |

| End | Thu, 04/17/2014 | 8:00 PM |

| | All day ☐ |

| View more options |

Figure 13-7: The Add Event screen.

Keeping events separate and private

When you have multiple calendars stored in one place (in this case, your phone), you might get confused when you want to add a new event. It can be even more confusing when you need to add the real event on one calendar and a placeholder on another.

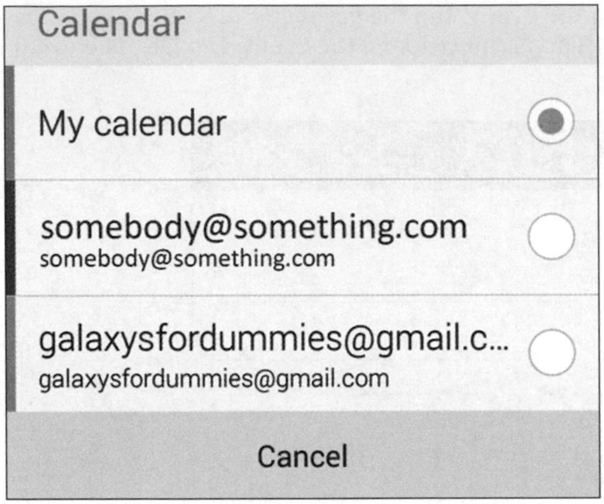

Calendar

My calendar ⊙

somebody@something.com ○
somebody@something.com

galaxysfordummies@gmail.c... ○
galaxysfordummies@gmail.com

Cancel

Figure 13-8: Choose a calendar.

Suppose your boss is a jerk, and to retain your sanity, you need to find a new job. You send your résumé to the archrival firm, Plan B, which has offices across town. Plan B is interested and wants you to interview at 3:00 p.m. next Tuesday. All good news.

The problem is that your current boss demands that you track your every move on the company calendaring system. His draconian management style is to berate people if they're not at their desks doing work if they're not at a scheduled meeting. (By the way, I am not making up this scenario.) You follow my drift. You don't want Snidely Whiplash trudging through your calendar, sniffing out your plans to exit stage left, and making life more miserable if Plan B doesn't work out.

Instead, you want to put a reasonable-sounding placeholder on your work calendar, while putting the real event on your personal calendar. You can easily do this from your HTC One Calendar app. When you're making the event, tell the phone where you want the event stored, making sure to keep each event exactly where it belongs. When you save the event, it's stored strictly on your phone or your personal Gmail account. Now create a new event (in this case, a phony doctor's appointment) on your work calendar.

After you save the event, it will appear forevermore on that calendar until you delete it. Just be sure to keep straight on which calendar you intend to store which event. The name of the calendar on which each event is stored appears under the Calendar heading.

On the Road Again: Taking Work on Your Phone

In This Chapter

▶ Using Mobile Office applications

▶ Navigating the Office applications in the cloud

▶ Sharing files using your phone

*W*hen you pick up your HTC One, you're holding as much computing power as was available in a high-end laptop five years ago — and a graphics processor that would have made a hard-core gamer envious. So it's not far-fetched to want to do some work with your Microsoft Office applications on your HTC One while you're away from your desk. Why not?

The HTC One actually doesn't allow you to leave your computer behind for good. The keyboard isn't great for typing an entire novel, for instance. What makes the most sense is to use your phone to view Office documents and make minor changes. Leave the hard-core creation and modification efforts to a full-size PC.

The Polaris Office 5 Suite, which you can download to your phone, lets you be productive on the road. In this chapter, I start with a little introduction on the basics, explore the tools, and explain how you can use them to your best advantage. Then I walk you through the Polaris Office app so you can know where everything is. Finally, I fill you in on file sharing, so you can get files on and off your phone and out into the world.

Editing Sheets

POLARIS® Office 5, you can create n~
~es or edit your worksh~

Preparing for Using Office Apps

Microsoft Office applications are the most popular apps for general-purpose business productivity. Virtually every business uses Microsoft Office or applications that can work with Microsoft file formats. For everything Microsoft Office, check out *Office 2013 For Dummies* or *Office 2010 For Dummies,* by Wallace Wang (Wiley).

As you're probably well aware, the heavy hitters are

- **Microsoft Word:** For creating and editing documents. These files end in .doc and .docx.

- **Microsoft Excel:** For managing spreadsheets, performing numerical analysis, and creating charts. These files end in .xls and .xlsx.

- **Microsoft PowerPoint:** For creating and viewing presentations. These files end in .ppt and .pptx.

The newest versions of Microsoft Office files are appended with .docx, .xlsx, and .pptx. Polaris can work with the older and newer formats. In general, however, more applications work with the older versions. You don't give up much by using the older version, but you do gain more compatibility with other people who aren't as current. Over time, the discrepancies become less of an issue as more people update to the newer format.

If you skip this section and don't have any software on your phone to open Office documents, you won't be able to read any Office documents attached to messages you receive on your phone. On the other hand, you may not want to be able to look at the documents until you're in the office.

Getting ahold of Office files

The next challenge: keeping track of the most recent version of whatever file you're working on. In the most basic scenario, you're working on a Microsoft Office file yourself. If you have a desktop PC, you're probably used to transferring files among different machines if you want to work on them in different locations, such as home or the office.

Here are your traditional options:

- **Removable media:** You use a thumb drive or disc to move the file from one PC to another.

- **Email:** You email the file from one PC to another.

> ✔ **Server:** You save a copy of your file from the first PC on a server that you can access from both the first and second PC.

The first option, unfortunately, is out. Your HTC One doesn't have a disc drive or a USB port for a thumb drive. You can use MicroSD cards for transferring music, along with the USB holder covered in Chapter 12. Frankly, this is enough of a hassle with music files that don't change that much. It's a nightmare for Office files that are changing all the time.

This leaves you with the second two options: using email or using a server. Sending and receiving Microsoft Office files as attachments with text or email messages is probably old hat by now. You receive the email, download the attachment, and work away. When you're done, you save the file to work on later, or you send it back to your PC. I go into more detail about this process later in this chapter.

The server option calls for a little more explanation. By the way, there are two fancy terms for this kind of computing. The first one is *cloud computing*. Readers of a certain age will recall this computing concept as *time-sharing*, but that name is out of fashion. Cloud computing is in vogue, so this is the terminology I shall use.

There is also an idea called a *VPN*, or *virtual private network*. This is fairly common in businesses. It's similar to cloud computing, but the "cloud" in this case is the company's computer system.

Cloud computing

File sharing is a basic part of Office app. The more Office files you store on the server, the better. It will do you little good if the files you want to see and change are safely stored on your PC, which you dutifully powered off to save energy.

The principle behind this service is that the server appears to your PC and your phone as if it were a drive or memory card directly connected to your machine. If you know how to copy files from, say, your PC hard drive to a USB thumb drive, you can use a server. You might not know which computer is doing the processing when you open a file. It could be your phone; it could also be a computer on the company network, or the server itself. Ultimately, you don't really care as long as it works fast and does what you want.

When you tap a filename that appears on your phone (which is comparable to double-clicking a filename on your PC), the file opens, and you can read and edit it. When you're done reading or editing, the file gets saved. This is the essence of cloud computing, and your phone can happily participate.

A popular online storage option, Dropbox, crops up in Chapter 1 and again in Chapter 9. In essence, Dropbox is a server that you can use for cloud computing. You need to sign up for free with the Dropbox service (at `www.dropbox.com/index`) to get access to its server. You need to register, but the good news is that anyone with a Gmail account automatically has a Dropbox account. Just use your email address and password, and you're set. Dropbox gives you multiple GB of storage for your files just for showing up.

And if you don't want to work with Dropbox, you have lots of other choices.

Using a VPN

The idea behind a VPN is that your phone and the company's data network set up a secret password. They know it's you because you entered your password. Any evildoers who see your information exchanges would see gibberish. Only your phone and the company computers know how to unscramble the gibberish.

As with checking your business email on your phone, make sure that your company is okay with you accessing files this way. In many cases, it's okay, but some companies have security policies that simply don't let you (or just anyone) have access to every piece of data that the company has ever had. I mean, you could be sitting in a competitor's office.

Reading and Editing Files with Your Phone

You can get Polaris Office Mobile Viewer from the Play Store for free if it's not already installed on your phone.

They ask you to register with them. It can be with your email account, Facebook, or LinkedIn. They just want to know who you are and that you are going to respect their stuff. That seems reasonable to me.

Creating a document

To introduce the process, I show you how to create a document on your phone:

1. **On your phone, open the app list and tap the Polaris Office 5 icon.**

2. **Accept the end user license agreement.**

   The Home screen appears, as shown in Figure 14-1.

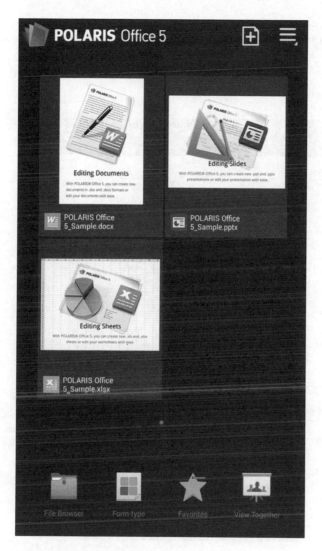

Figure 14-1: Polaris on your phone.

3. **Tap the icon for the file type you wish to create**:

- *Editing Documents:* Open a blank sheet in Word format (.doc).

- *Editing Sheets:* Open a blank spreadsheet in Excel spreadsheet format (.xls).

- *Editing Slides:* Open a blank presentation in PowerPoint format (.ppt).

Tapping any icon brings up a screen like the one in Figure 14-2 — a Word document that describes how to use the app. The details of editing are described in this document.

Word Icon

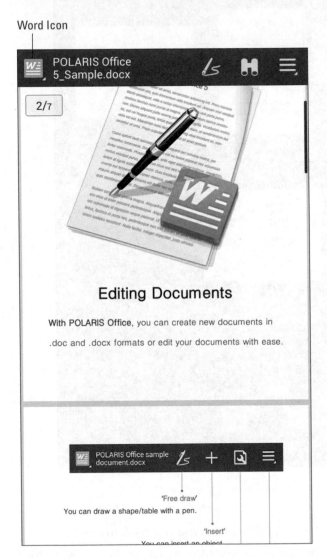

Figure 14-2: Viewing your Polaris document on your phone.

4. **Tap the Word icon in the upper-left corner to begin the process to save the document.**

   Doing so brings up the options, as shown in Figure 14-3. In this case, your only option is to save this file in your phone's memory or on the MicroSD card on your phone (if one is installed). If it helps you keep track of which revision of the file you have on your phone, you can rename it to, say, filename-phone.doc. More on your other options in a moment.

Figure 14-3: The Save As option on the Polaris My Docs page.

5. **To save this document, tap the diskette icon at upper right.**

   The diskette might indeed be a relic of earlier PC technology, but it still widely means Save.

   You follow the same basic process for files in the other formats. If you want to keep this file on your phone forever, you're set. However, read on if you want to do something more with it.

Sending an Office file as an attachment

After a file is saved, it's safe to send it to your home PC or to another PC. When you're ready to email the document, do the following, which is the same for Word, Excel, and PowerPoint documents:

1. **Tap the Word icon.**

2. **Tap Send Email.**

   You see Send Email, Original, and PDF options, as shown in Figure 14-4.

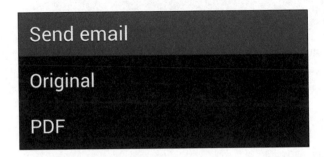

Send email

Original

PDF

Figure 14-4: Email file options.

3. **Tap an option.**

   If you send it as a PDF, you can't edit it. Tap Original to send it as a Word document.

4. **Type in the contact or email address.**

   This brings up a blank email screen with your document automatically included as an attachment. This screen is shown in Figure 14-5.

5. **Type an email address in the To text box. Add a subject and a message if you want.**

   If you want the document on your PC, simply address it to yourself.

6. **Tap Send.**

   The miracle of wireless communication zips the document to the intended recipient.

The formatting of the document on your phone might not be exactly the same as it is when it reappears on your PC. Save yourself time and don't try to format a document on your HTC One.

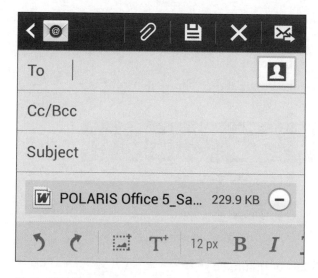

Figure 14-5: The email screen with your doc set as an attachment.

Managing Office documents with a server

Regardless of how you send an Office file to or from your phone, the creation and editing steps are the same. The steps in the preceding section cover the basics. You can do basic editing with the simplified icons at the bottom of the screen.

The next step is to work with files stored on a server. As I mention earlier, you can work with any server. The easiest way to describe the process is to start from the server's point of view. Suppose you're writing the great American novel on your PC, but then you want to put it on your phone so you can review it and maybe make some minor edits. The first thing you do is move the file to your Dropbox server from your PC. Figure 14-6 is what it looks like on your desktop PC.

Figure 14-6: Dropbox on a PC.

This should look familiar. Here are the steps to view and edit this document on your phone:

1. **Tap the Dropbox icon.**

   Doing so brings up the screen shown in Figure 14-7.

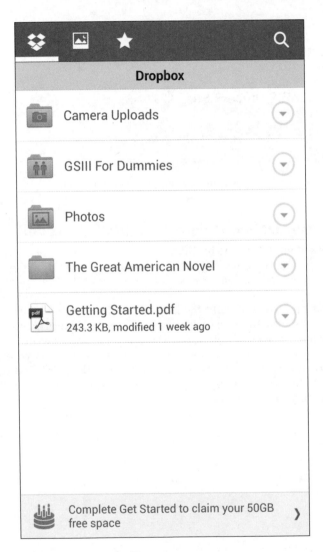

Figure 14-7: Dropbox on the phone.

2. **Tap the folder that has the file you want.**

   In this case, it's the folder titled *The Great American Novel*, as shown in Figure 14-8.

Figure 14-8: The file in the Dropbox folder.

3. **Tap the filename to open the file.**

   The image in Figure 14-9 shows my novel so far.

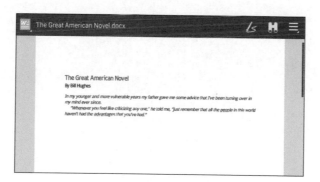

Figure 14-9: The document open in Polaris.

4. **Read or edit the file as desired.**

5. **When you're done, tap the Word icon.**

   A menu opens.

6. **Tap Save.**

   This saves any changes you've made back to the file, which is stored on Dropbox.

This process works with any Microsoft Office file format. It works with cloud servers other than Dropbox too. It can work the same way with your VPN at the office.

Talking with Google Now

In This Chapter

▶ Telling your phone to make a call

▶ Dictating an email or text

▶ Doing a web search without typing

*E*very science fiction movie worth its salt predicts a world where we speak to computers rather than typing in data. The reality is that there are many technical obstacles to voice recognition perfectly interpreting your verbal instructions. That doesn't stop us from having some fun in the meantime, however! Google Now, an app within the Google Search app, can handle some basic functions, including making a phone call, sending an email or a text, searching the Internet, or even updating your Facebook status.

You may love this capability, or you may find it to be a gimmick and not very useful. Try it.

You may have heard of Siri on Apple's iPhone. Siri responds to questions you ask. The Google Now app is the same idea, only it responds to "OK, Google."

Look Ma! No Hands!

To get started, tap the Google icon. This brings up the screens shown in Figure 15-1. The first screen introduces Google Now, while the second lets you opt out if this whole intelligent agent thing seems creepy. In that case, Google Search works like it does on your desktop (in other words, bo-ring).

First Google Now Screen

Second Google Now Screen

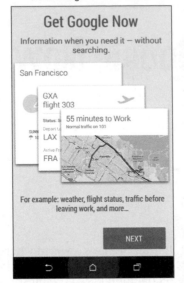
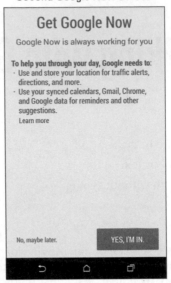

Figure 15-1: Google Now permission screens.

If you are daring and agree to use Google Now, you see a screen similar to Figure 15-2, but customized for your local area.

Now ask for what you want. Say you want to call someone.

In the old days, high-end cellular phones would require you to train the voice-recognition software to understand the basics of how you speak. No more. Just tell it who you want to call, by saying, "Call Ludwig."

Be ready. In just a moment, it calls Ludwig. It's that easy. Almost.

First, Google is very aware, almost hyper-aware, of how sensitive this information is. The first time you access information on your phone, such as your contacts list or calendar, it asks permission. Go ahead and grant it if you want to use Google Now.

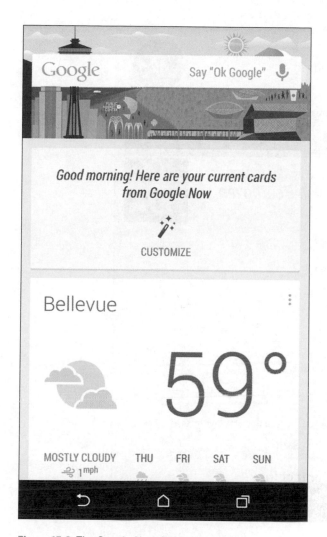

Figure 15-2: The Google Now Start screen.

Since you only know one Ludwig, your phone will respond in a somewhat mechanical female voice, "Calling Ludwig Von Beethoven." See Figure 15-3.

Figure 15-3: The Google Now calling screen.

In a few moments, you 're connected so you can chat.

Next, say you want to call Bill Boyce. Either tap the microphone silhouette in the search box or say, "OK, Google." Then you say "Call Bill."

If you know one Bill, it will call that Bill. If you know several people named Bill, your phone prompts you which Bill you want to call. This is reasonable. The first time you ask, how would it know which one you mean?

It's better to say "Call Bill Boyce." Within a moment, his phone rings.

A few pointers for using Google Now. If you hesitate, Google Now assumes that you aren't ready to talk and goes into a sleep mode. To wake it up, just say "Hi Google." It wakes up, ready to resume listening.

I get to the list of things that work with Google Now soon. For now, try a few of its simple yet valuable capabilities.

Dictating a Text

To send a text, say the words, "Send Ludwig a text."

It responds with the contact and asks, "What is that message?" Go ahead and say what you would have typed. Google Now converts your words into a message. It displays what it thinks you said in a box similar to Figure 15-4.

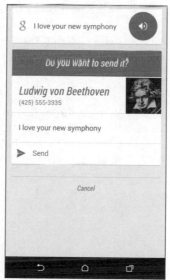

Figure 15-4: The Google Now texting response boxes.

Read it before you send it. Google Now is imperfect. If it is correct, just say "Send" and off it goes. What could be easier? If it is not right, either manually edit the text or say, "Don't send." Google Now will let you try again.

Preparing to Work with Google Now

You can ask Google Now to do all kinds of things on your phone:

- Telling you the time
- Setting an alarm
- Turning Wi-Fi on or off
- Telling you the weather forecast
- Setting a countdown timer
- Recording your voice
- Opening an app
- Playing a playlist
- Adding an event to your schedule
- Finding a local restaurant, store, or public location
- Navigating to an address or location

All you need to do is ask, and Google Now does a good job finding what you want. For example, you can ask for a nearby McDonald's, and Google Now comes back with the options as if I had entered McDonald's into a Google Search.

Then you can ask it for directions to the McDonald's you choose. This request causes Google Now to hand you over to your preferred navigation application, bringing up a screen like the one shown in Figure 15-5. Now all you need to do is drive there safely and enjoy!

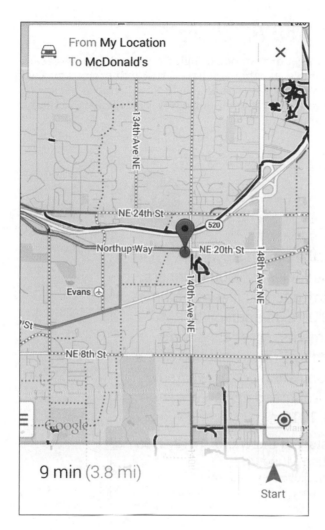

Figure 15-5: Navigation to the location you requested.

Searching the Web by Voice

These functions get pretty cool. Google Now can do some research on your behalf. For example, say that you have a research project, and want to know, "When was the War of 1812?" Ask Google Now. It comes back with the answer shown in Figure 15-6. Granted, Google Now doesn't see the scathingly witty humor in this question.

Figure 15-6: Google Now's response to "When was the War of 1812?"

Changing Settings on Google Now

Google Now is eager to be helpful. You can help it be helpful by giving it some information. Google Now refers to this information as *cards* and they include basics such as your home or work address.

You can get to these cards by flicking to the bottom of the Google Now Home screen. You will see the icons shown in Figure 15-7: a knot tied to a finger, a sparkly magic wand, and the ever-present three vertical dots.

Figure 15-7: Google Now's settings categories.

▸ The **hand with the piece of string on a finger** are reminders. You can ask Google Now to remind you of important events. It is cool, but not what we are here for.

▸ The **magic wand** is where you provide your *cards* — personalized information about you. You can choose Sports, Stocks, Places, or Everything Else. For example, you can put your home address into Places. That makes it easier for you to say something like "Give me directions home." Tapping the magic wand brings up the screen in Figure 15-8. The Everything Else category is shown in Figure 15-9. The number to the right is the number of customizations you have stored.

▸ The **three dots** bring you to the Google Now settings. If you like this feature, you can customize many of the default settings, like whether you want it to block certain words. This feature can come in handy if you use Google Now to send texts and do not bother to check them carefully.

Once you have added the settings that are meaningful to you, Google keeps an eye out for new stories relating to your stock picks and sports teams. Give it a try and see if you like the information that you get. For example, Google Now knows that I can get on an interstate highway to go home. If I usually get around by walking, Google Now wouldn't put me on the interstate if I wanted to walk to Boise.

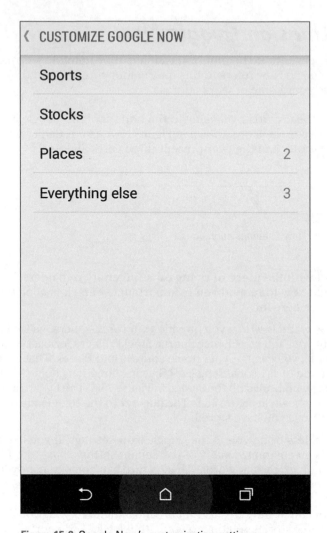

Figure 15-8: Google Now's customization settings.

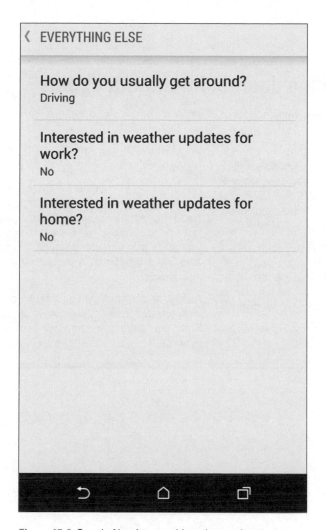

Figure 15-9: Google Now's everything else settings.

007 with a degree: Intelligent agents

Among computer scientists, Google Now is called an *intelligent agent*.

Google Now is a pretty darn good implementation of intelligent-agent technology. It's about as good as you can get when you're using many of the basic functions of your HTC One. The list of things you can do with Google Now includes a pretty long list of the primary capabilities.

Even so, the truth is that this technology is not perfected yet. If you don't want to use an intelligent agent until it's perfected, no one could blame you. Before you dismiss this function as a gimmick, however, think about a few things:

✔ Normal speech equals about 150 words per minute.

✔ A fast typist can type at 90 words per minute.

✔ Most people can write 30 words per minute by hand.

You and I may be better off if we can adjust our expectations. If you use Google Now for standard commands, it performs remarkably fast and accurately. You will get to say to your grandkids that you were among the pioneers who used intelligent agents before it was mainstream.

As long as evil intelligent agent HAL, from *2001: A Space Odyssey,* never comes to pass, it's likely that this technology will become more common.

the
part of
tens

Enjoy an additional Part of Tens at www.dummies.com/extras/htconem8.

In this part . . .

- Get the most out of your phone.
- Protect yourself if you lose your phone.
- Avoid losing your phone in the first place.
- Discover what features will be coming in future versions.

Ten Ways to Make Your Phone Totally Yours

A smartphone is a very personal device. From the moment you take it out of the box and strip off the packaging, you begin to make it yours. By the end of the first day, even though millions of HTC Ones may have been sold, there's no other phone just like yours.

This is the case because of the phone calls you make and because of all the options you can set on the phone and all the information you can share over the web. Your contacts, music files, downloaded videos, texts, and favorites make your phone a unique representation of who you are and what's important to you.

Even with all this "you" on your phone, this chapter covers ten ways to further customize your phone beyond what you have already explored. I also zero in on one way that I suggest you *don't* modify your phone!

Using a Charging Dock

The HTC One comes with a charging cable and the transformer. It is straightforward to put your phone on a desk or your nightstand to charge. At the same time, you have one of the nicest-looking smartphones on the market. It looks better when you prop it up.

It also will sound better when playing music. The HTC One comes with better built-in speakers than any smartphone on the market. Its sound is clear and powerful. All the specs show that this is *the* phone for music lovers.

Putting your phone in a docking station (aka *charging dock*) will help you see the information on your phone and make your phone sound better.

Driving in Style with a Car Docking Station

Your phone has a number of great navigation tools, so you'll want to use them in your car. You could always put your phone on the seat next to you, but that's for amateurs. Instead, offer your phone a place of honor with a car docking station. It makes accessing your phone while you drive safer and easier. Some see getting a car mount as a luxury, but my view is that if you need to upgrade your navigation software, you need a vehicle mount.

If you're using the Map app to get somewhere, let someone else drive. Also, put away the docking station when you park. Even an empty docking station is a lure for a thief.

Figure 16-1 shows a generic vehicle mount for the HTC One. This puts your phone where you can see it *and* what is going on around you. It costs about $35, and you can get it at your carrier's store, RadioShack, Best Buy, or online at Amazon.com.

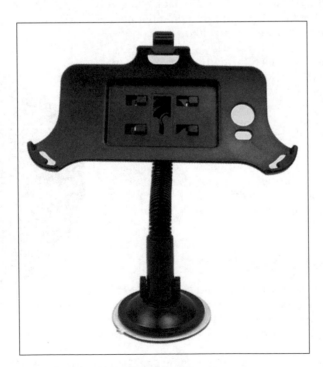

Figure 16-1: A generic HTC vehicle navigation mount.

Some vehicle mount brands are made specifically for the HTC One. Others are made to fit multiple devices. You may want to get a generic mount if multiple people (with various types of phones) use your car.

Cruising with a Bluetooth Car Speaker

You still want to take calls from your phone. In that case, it is a great idea to use a Bluetooth car speaker. It is easier and safer than looking at the screen while you drive.

By the way, you may have gotten the idea that I am concerned about your safety when you're using your phone. True, but I'm more concerned with *my* safety when you're using your phone. I would like you to have a Bluetooth speaker in your car when driving in my neighborhood, if you please.

Some cars have a built-in Bluetooth speaker that connects to a microphone somewhere on the dash as well as to your car speakers. It's smart enough to sense when there's an incoming call and mutes your music in response. If you don't have such a fancy setup, there are lots of good options for car speakers. An example of a visor-mounted speaker appears in Figure 16-2.

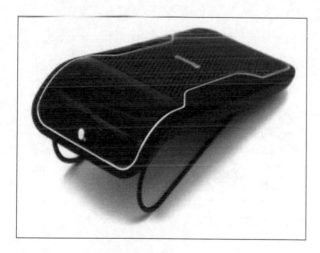

Figure 16-2: Bluetooth car speaker.

Making a Statement with Wraps

The HTC One is attractive, but if you want to spruce it up even more, you can get a wrapping (such as from Skinit, www.skinit.com). There are designs to express more of what is important to you. As a side benefit, they can protect your phone from minor scratches.

Figure 16-3 shows some design options for a skin. If you're not crazy about their designs, you can make your own with images of your own choosing. Just be sure that you have the rights to use the images!

It comes with cut-outs for speakers, plugs, microphones, and cameras specifically for the HTC One. Putting the skin on is similar to putting on a decal, although the material has a little give. The skin material and adhesive is super high-tech and has enough give to help klutzes like me (who struggle with placing regular decals) fit the nooks and crannies.

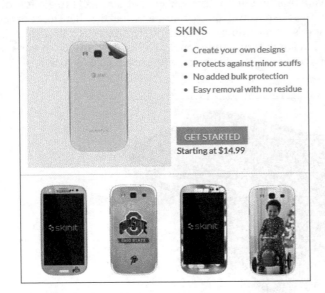

Figure 16-3: Some sample Skinit designs.

Maximizing Shortcuts from Home

You won't spend much time there, but your extended Home screen is critical to your phone experience. Ideally, you keep a tidy group of shortcut icons on the *extended Home screens* (the five or so screens that appear when you turn on your phone or tap the Home button). This is probably as likely as keeping your house immaculate day in and day out. Fortunately, keeping your Home screen clutter-free is easier than cleaning up in the real world.

You can add shortcuts to the Home screens for the following things. Read more about how in Chapter 2.

- ✓ Specific contacts so you can bring up the person you want to call or text.
- ✓ Text addresses so you can just tap and type your message.
- ✓ Directions to a favorite place.
- ✓ Folders where you've stored Microsoft Office files.
- ✓ Apps or games that you use frequently.

Tap the Manage Home Screen Panels link to get started:

- ✓ **Add shortcuts** until the pages of your Home screen are full. Adding a shortcut involves pressing and holding the app icon from the apps list.
- ✓ **Add more pages to your extended Home screen** by pressing and holding an open space on any Home screen. You get a silhouette, as seen in Figure 16-4.
- ✓ **Move among your extended Home screens** by flicking left or right.
- ✓ **Remove a Home screen** by centering it and tapping the link that says Remove.
- ✓ **Make any page the main Home screen** by tapping the link that says Set as Home. Finally, you can add more screens by tapping the plus sign at the right.

Figure 16-4: Managing your Home screen.

You Look Mahvelous: Custom Screen Images

Tap the Choose Wallpaper link and make your selection.

In addition to the shortcuts on your Home screen, you can change the background:

✔ Any picture from your Gallery can be stretched across the seven Home screens. (Read more about Gallery in Chapter 9.)

✔ Choose a neutral background image (similar to those on PCs) from the wallpaper Gallery. Figure 16-5 shows background images.

✔ Opt for a live wallpaper that responds to your finger. The live wallpaper that subtly reacts to the screen is more interesting than, say, a static picture of a colorful bowl of fruit. Check out some and see if they capture your imagination.

Figure 16-5: Wallpaper samples.

Personalizing Your App List

The next most important area for enjoying your phone is your application list. The advantage of customizing is that you can hide the icons of the apps you do not want to see, but for whatever reason, you do not want to delete from your phone.

Depending on your phone, you have these options for personalizing this list:

✔ Applications in an order you customize.

✔ Applications in alphabetic order. The advantage of having your apps in alphabetic order is that you learn over time where they are.

✔ Application that you used most recently. If you have a lot of apps, it may be easiest to sort the list according to your most recent use.

From the apps list, tap the link that says Apps in the upper-left corner. You see a screen like the one in Figure 16-6.

Using HTC One as a TV Remote

Your phone can talk to a long list of Bluetooth devices. It can also talk to your TV like as a smart remote control! This isn't just a universal remote control. The TV app can help you find new shows that you may like based upon your preferences.

You need to set it up to get the full benefit of being able to control your entire suite of TVs, set-top boxes, and stereos from your phone. This app will know where you are (so it knows what local programming is available), but it asks where you get your TV service and the equipment at your home.

To get started, tap the HTC Sense TV app icon (the box sending off radio waves). From there, you answer some questions. You also need to take some steps with your phone according to the exact brand and model of each piece of AV equipment in your home. If you have ever set up a universal remote, the steps will be familiar. You tell HTC Sense the brand of the device, and your phone asks you to tell it when the device turns on or off. As you watch your shows, this app learns what shows you have watched and, over time, can make suggestions.

Figure 16-6: App sorting options.

Checking Out the HTC One Mini+

Your HTC One is cool, but sometimes you want to use a simpler gadget. HTC offers you an option: the HTC Mini+. It connects to your HTC One (M8) and you can use it to make calls, control your TV, and get messages.

Okay, this is really gilding the lily — but it is a cool option for the HTC One owner with everything.

Keeping Pace with Health and Fitness Monitors

I know you're going to buy a pedometer. You're going to start being more careful about your health. You can use your smartphone to help. Using Bluetooth, you can connect medical sensors to track health-related measurements like blood pressure, blood sugar levels, or oxygen levels in your bloodstream.

Each solution is unique, but in general, an app connects with a sensor. This sensor is often attached to your wrist for the sake of convenience. This app monitors your status. If you should exceed a preset number, the application tells your phone what to do. If you're healthy and this sensor is for fitness, your phone can track your progress.

Your status may be sent to a caregiver at a suitable priority. For example, if your heart rate is a little elevated, the HTC One could send a low-priority message to your doctor. If your condition is urgent, your phone could text a caregiver or specially trained staff member.

If you use these features, rest assured that you *will* need to acknowledge a library of disclaimers. At the end of the day, however, the goal is to increase the chance of getting good information to someone who can do something about it.

Fitness buffs can use the Onyx II wireless pulse oximeter from Nonin. Someone with diabetes can use the FORA G31 Blood Glucose Monitoring System from TaiDoc Technology Corporation to measure blood-sugar levels. You can see the system in Figure 16-7.

You gain two advantages by using applications like these:

- **Automatic recordkeeping.** You're probably human, as in, "only human." And, as an imperfect human being, you don't always record your results. Your phone solves this little imperfection by always recording your results. Plus, your phone probably has better handwriting than you.

- **Who ya gonna call? Your phone knows.** Your phone is set up to send the results to a tracking application that a health specialist monitors. The specialists have the knowledge and experience to flag imminent problems or promising trends. This arrangement is much more sophisticated than what is available from standalone monitors.

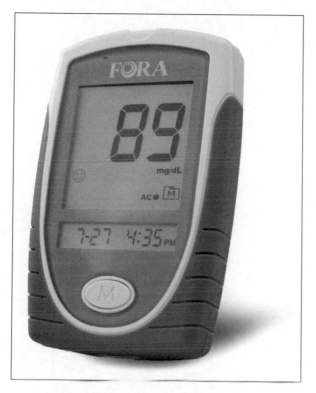

Figure 16-7: The FORA G31 Blood Glucose Monitoring System from TaiDoc.

Ten Ways to Make Your Phone Secure

In This Chapter

▶ Keeping your phone in one piece

▶ Avoiding losing your phone in the first place

▶ Protecting yourself if you do lose your phone

*B*ack in the "old" days, it sure was frustrating to have your regular-feature phone lost or stolen. You would lose all your contacts, call history, and texts. Even if you backed up all of your contacts, you would have to re-enter them in your new phone. What a hassle.

The good news is that your smartphone saves all your contacts on your Gmail account. The bad news is that, unless you take the steps outlined in this chapter, evildoers could conceivably drain your bank account, get you fired, or even have you arrested.

Do I have your attention? Think of what would happen if someone were to get access to your PC at home or at work. He or she could wreak havoc on your life. A malevolent prankster could send an email from your work email address under your name. It could be a rude note to the head of your company. It could give phony information about a supposedly imminent financial collapse of your company to the local newspaper. It could be a threat to the U.S. president, generating a visit from the Secret Service.

Here's the deal: If you have done anything with your smartphone as described in this book past Chapter 3, I expect you'll want to take steps to protect your smartphone. This is the burden of having a well-connected device. Fortunately, most of the steps are simple and straightforward.

Use a Good Case and Screen Cover

The HTC One is sleek and beautiful. Plus, the front is made of Gorilla Glass from Corning. This stuff is durable and scratch resistant. So why am I telling you to cover all this up? It's like buying a fancy dress for a prom or wedding and wearing a coat all night. Yup. It's necessary for safe mobile computing.

Speaking from personal experience, dropping a phone on concrete can break the glass and some of the innards. This can happen if you simply keep your phone in a pocket.

There are lots of choices for cases. The most popular are made of silicone, plastic, or leather. There are different styles that meet your needs from many manufacturers. Otterbox is a brand that makes a series of cases for multiple levels of protection. Some examples are seen in Figure 17-1.

Figure 17-1: Otterbox cases for the HTC One.

You don't just use a good case so you can hand off a clean used phone to the next lucky owner. A case protects your phone against damage. If your phone is damaged, you have to mail it or bring it to a repair shop. The problem is that many people who bring their phones in for repair don't wipe the personal information off their devices. You really hope that the repair shop can pop off the broken piece, pop on a new one, and send you on your way.

It's rarely that easy. Typically, you need to leave your phone in the hands of strangers for some period of time. For the duration of the repair, said strangers have access to the information on your phone.

The good news is that most workers who repair phones are professional and will probably delete any information from the phone before they start fixing it. (And hopefully you recently backed up all your smartphone files.)

However, do you want to take that chance? Do you want the hassle of getting a new phone? Probably not, so invest in a good case and screen cover.

Put It on Lockdown

The most basic effort you can take to protect your phone is to put some kind of a screen lock on your phone.

If you're connected to a corporate network, the company may have a policy that specifies what you must do to access your corporate network. Otherwise you have several choices, listed here in increasing degrees of security:

- ✔ Unlock with a simple swipe across the screen
- ✔ Show the lock screen, but not offer any additional security
- ✔ Unlock with a pattern that you swipe on the screen
- ✔ Unlock with facial recognition
- ✔ Unlock with a PIN
- ✔ Unlock with a password
- ✔ Encrypt everything on your phone

You can select any of the first five options in the Lock Screen option in Settings. Encrypting everything on your phone has some serious implications, so I describe it in more detail later in the chapter, in the "Encrypt Your Device" section.

If you want to choose one of the first five options, here's what you do:

1. **From the apps screen, tap the settings (gear) icon.**

   This is probably old hat by now.

2. **Scroll down to the Security link and tap it.**

   Tapping it brings up the screen in Figure 17-2.

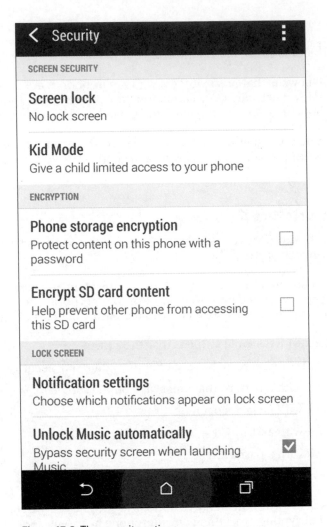

Figure 17-2: The security options.

For reasons that sort of make sense, your phone uses some terminology that can be confusing. To clarify, the term *Screen Lock* is an option you can select to prevent unauthorized users from getting into your phone. The term *Lock Screen* is short for the action of locking your screen or enabling the Screen Lock option.

3. **Tap the Screen Lock link.**

Tapping it brings up the options seen in Figure 17-3. Each option prompts you through what it needs before establishing your security selection.

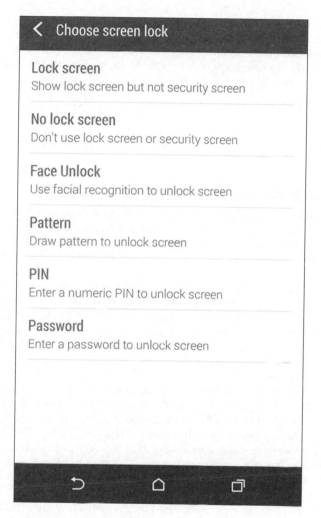

Figure 17-3: The screen lock options.

Preparing for your screen lock option

Regardless of what screen lock you choose, I recommend that you have ready the following choices at hand:

- A PIN. A *PIN* is a series of numbers. In this case, the PIN is four digits.

- A password. A *password* is a series of numbers, upper- and lowercase letters, and sometimes special characters, and is typically longer than four characters. A PIN is pretty secure, but a password is usually more secure.

✔ An unlock pattern. This is a design that you draw with your finger on a nine-dot screen. You do not need to use all the dots. The minimum number of dots you must touch is four. The upper limit is nine because you can only touch each dot once. As long as you can remember your pattern, feel free to be creative.

✔ A preference regarding facial recognition, pattern, PIN, or password.

These options are in order of convenience (at least in my opinion, which may or may not be yours). This order *isn't* the same as the level of security.

Selecting among the screen lock options

The first option, unlocking your phone with a swipe, fools exactly no one and doesn't slow anyone down. Rather than just having the Home screen appear, your phone tells you to swipe your finger on the screen to get to the Home screen. This is about as secure as waving at an intruder. Keep going.

Although these options are cool, I recommend drawing out a pattern as the minimum screen-lock option. (Tap the Pattern option.) The phone asks you to enter your pattern, and then asks you to enter it again. It then asks you to enter a PIN in case you forget your pattern. *Use a PIN you can remember a long time from now.* You only need this pin if you forget your pattern. That is a very rare situation for most of us.

The next more secure option is to use facial recognition. It is usually handy. Most of us carry our face with us wherever we go. Using it is convenient, unless you rob banks for a living and wear a full ski mask much of the time. However, you do need to put your faith in the technology. Personally, I have had good experience, and you always have the option to use the alternative password. I suggest trying it, and seeing if you are comfortable with how it works. If not, just come back to this screen and reset your options.

The next two options are the PIN and password. They are straightforward for anyone that has used a PC for more than a few days or has an ATM card. These two options are pretty darn secure, but only as long as you avoid the obvious choices. If you insist upon using 0000 or 1111 or the word *password* as your password, don't waste your time. It's standard operating procedure within the typical den of thieves to try these sequences first.

If, someday, you forget your pattern, your PIN, or your password, the only option is to do a complete reset of your phone back to original factory settings. In such a case, all your texts and stored files will be lost. Try to avoid this fate: Remember your pattern, PIN, or password.

At the top end of the spectrum is encrypting your device. To use this option, it insists that you also use a password.

Encrypt Your Device

This is the last and most secure option for protecting your device. It's an exceptionally secure option: It scrambles every file on your phone into gibberish, which it rapidly descrambles when you need the information. This sounds great; in practice, however, there are some important considerations to think about.

- All this scrambling and descrambling takes processing power away from other things, such as running the apps. The loss is hardly noticeable in most cases — your phone is awash in processing power — but you never know when it might come back to bite you.

- You can never switch your phone back to non-encrypted use. With the screen lock options, you can use a PIN for a while, and then switch back to the pattern if you want. Not so with the encryption option. You will never, ever, ever, ever, get it back together. If you encrypt your phone and then forget your password, your phone is *bricked*. In effect, its only future use would be in house construction; you won't be able to use it as a smartphone anymore.

If *you're sure* you're sure that encryption is for you, have your password ready, the battery at 80 percent or higher, and an hour set aside when you don't need to use your phone:

1. **From the apps screen, tap the settings icon.**

2. **Scroll down and tap the Security link.**

   Doing so brings up the options shown back in Figure 17-2.

3. **Tap the Encrypt Device option.**

   This brings up the screen shown in Figure 17-4. (See. I did not make this up!)

4. **Enter a password.**

   This time, the password must include at least six characters with at least one number. In this case, the password "password1" is also off the table. This is the second-most-common lousy password that thieves routinely try.

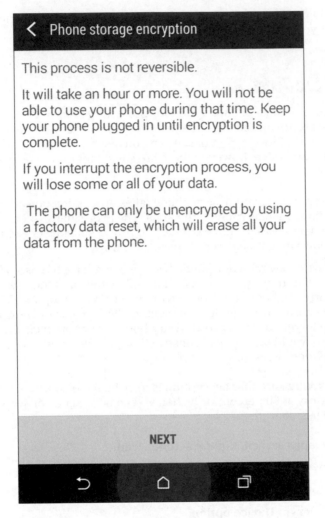

Figure 17-4: The encryption warning screen.

Be Careful with Bluetooth

Chapter 3 looks at syncing your phone with Bluetooth devices. It doesn't mention the potential for security risk at that point. I am mentioning it now. Perhaps the greatest vulnerability your phone faces is called *bluejacking*, which involves using some simple tricks to gain access to your phone via Bluetooth.

Big Brother

Some people are concerned that people with a radio scanner can listen in on their voice calls. This was possible, but not easy, in the early days of cellular phone use. Your HTC One can only use digital systems, so picking your conversation out of the air is practically impossible.

Some people are concerned that a radio scanner and a computer can pick up your data

connection. It's not that simple. Maybe the NSA could get some of your data that way using complicated supercomputing algorithms, but it's much easier for thieves and pranksters to use wired communications to access the accounts of the folks who use 0000 as their PIN and *password* as their password.

Do a test: Turn on Bluetooth the next time you're in a public place such as a coffee shop, a restaurant, or a train station. Tap the button that makes you visible to all Bluetooth devices, and then tap Scan. While your Bluetooth device is visible, you'll see all the other Bluetooth devices in your vicinity. You'll probably find lots of them. If not, try this at an airport. Wow!

If you were trying to pair with another Bluetooth device, you'd be asked whether you're willing to accept connection to that device. In this case, you are not. However, a hacker will see that you are open for pairing, and take this opportunity to use the PIN 0000 to make a connection.

When you're actively pairing, your Bluetooth device won't accept an unknown device's offer to pair. But if your device is both *unpaired and visible,* hackers can fool your Bluetooth device and force a connection.

After a connection is established, all your information is available to the hackers to use as they will. Here are the steps to protect yourself:

✔ **Don't pair your phone to another Bluetooth device in a public place.** Believe it or not, crooks go to public places to look for phones in pairing mode. When they pair with a phone, they look for interesting data to steal. It would be nice if these people had more productive hobbies, like parkour or searching for Bigfoot. However, as long as these folks are out there, it is safer to pair your Bluetooth device in a not-so-public place.

✔ **Make sure that you know the name of the device with which you want to pair.** You should only pair with that device. Decline if you are not sure or if other Bluetooth devices offer to connect.

✔ **Shorten the default time-out setting.** The default is that you will be visible for two minutes. However, you can go into the settings and change the Visible Time-Out option to whatever you want. Make this time shorter than two minutes. *Don't set it to Never Time Out.* This is like leaving the windows open and the keys in the ignition on your Cadillac Escalade.

✔ **From time to time, check the names of the devices that are paired to your device.** If you don't recognize the name of a device, click the settings icon to the right of the unfamiliar name and unpair it. Some damage may have been done by the intruder, but with any luck you've nipped it in the bud.

Here's an important point: When handled properly, Bluetooth is as secure as can be. However, a few mistakes can open you up to human vermin with more technical knowledge than common sense. Avoid these mistakes and you can safely enjoy this capability.

Protect Against Malware

One of the main reasons people write apps for Android is that Google doesn't have an onerous pre-approval process for a new app to be placed in the Play Store. This is unlike the Apple App Store or Microsoft Windows Phone Store, where each app must be validated. Many developers prefer to avoid bureaucracy.

At least in theory, this attracts more developers to do more stuff for Android phones. However, this approach does expose users like you and me to the potential for malware that can, inadvertently or intentionally, do things that are not advertised. Some of these "things" may be minor annoyances, or they could really mess up your phone (for openers).

Market forces, in the form of negative feedback, are present to kill apps that are badly written or are meant to steal your private data. However, this informal safeguard works only after some poor soul has experienced problems — such as theft of personal information — and reported it.

Rather than simply avoiding new apps, you can download apps designed to protect the information on your phone.

These apps are available from many of the firms that make antivirus software for your PC. Importantly, many of these antivirus applications are free. If you want a nicer interface and some enhanced features, you can pay a few dollars, but this is not necessary. Examples include NG Mobile Security and Antivirus, Lookout Security and Antivirus, Kaspersky Mobile Security, and Norton Security Antivirus. If you have downloaded an app that has malicious software, these apps will stop that app.

Don't Download Apps from Just Anywhere

Another way to avoid malware is to download mobile software only from trustworthy websites. This book has focused exclusively on the Google Play Store. You can download Android apps for your phone from a number of other reputable sites, including PocketGear and MobiHand.

Keep in mind that these stores are always on the lookout to withdraw applications that include malicious software. Google uses an internally developed solution they call Bouncer to check for malicious software and remove it from the Play Store. Other mobile software distribution companies have their own approaches to addressing this problem. The problem is that policing malicious software is a hit-or-miss proposition.

As a rule, you should hesitate to download an Android application unless you know where it has been. You are safest if you restrict your app shopping to reputable companies. Be very skeptical of any other source of an Android application.

By the way, your phone won't let you download from any of these sites without you giving it explicit permission. If you want to download from some other site besides the Google Play Store, you have to check the right box. Under Security in the Settings folder (look at Figure 17-2), there is a link called Unknown Sources. See Figure 17-5. When Unknown Sources is *unchecked,* you can't download apps from any source other than the Google Play Store.

This may be overkill. They are many highly reputable stores. However, it would be impractical for Google to distinguish which ones are good or evil. They just make sure that you know that they aren't responsible if you choose to leave the safety of their store.

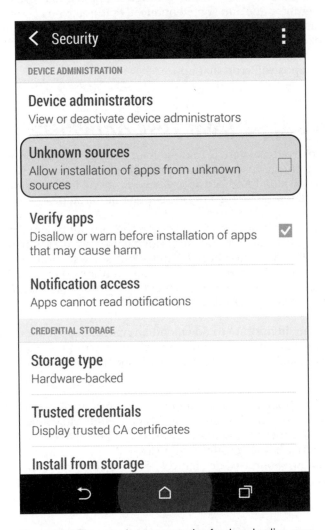

Figure 17-5: The security screen option for downloading apps.

Buy Antivirus Software

Rather than simply avoiding new apps from non-Google Play stores, you can download apps to protect the information on your phone. These are available from many of the firms that make antivirus software for your PC. Importantly, many of these antivirus applications are free. If you want a nicer interface and some enhanced features, you can pay. This is really a low cost way to have insurance.

Just like with malware-killing software, examples include NG Mobile Security and Antivirus, Lookout Security and Antivirus, Kaspersky Mobile Security, and Norton Security Antivirus.

Back Up Your Phone

As a responsible PC user, I'm sure that you back up your data on a daily basis. That way, if your PC should have a catastrophic failure, you can easily rebuild your system without trouble.

Yeah, right. The fact is that most of us are pretty lazy on our personal PCs. Most people back up PCs only on occasion.

Have you considered backing up your phone? Although much of your information is accessible through your Gmail account, you'll still need to rebuild your connections and re-enter your passwords.

The good news is that it is really easy. In Settings, tap Backup & Reset. This is seen in Figure 17-6. If the option Back Up My Data is checked, you're done. If it isn't checked, and you want to be backed up, tap the check box. Your Gmail account is the backup account.

If you need to restore your phone, tap Automatic Restore and follow the instructions. This could not be easier.

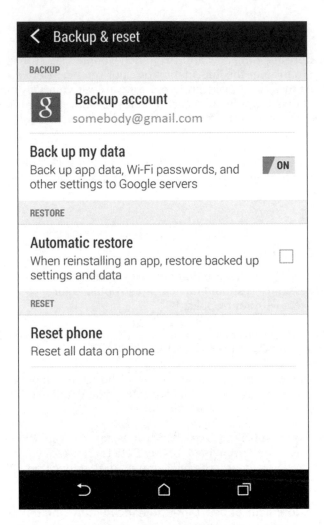

Figure 17-6: The Backup & Reset screen.

Rescue Your Phone When It Gets Lost

There are apps that help you find your phone. Here are a few "lost it" scenarios and some possible solutions for your quandary:

✏ *You know that you lost your phone somewhere in your house. You would try calling your own number, but it's set to Vibrate Only mode.*

If you know that your phone is in your house, the accuracy of GPS isn't savvy enough to tell you whether it's lost between the seat cushions of your couch or in the pocket of your raincoat. That's where the Remote Ring feature comes in handy.

Remote Ring: By sending a text to your phone (with the code that you pre-programmed when you set up this service), your phone will ring on its loudest setting, even if you have the ringer set to Vibrate Only.

✔ *You lost your phone while traveling, and have no idea whether you left it in a taxi or at airport security.*

Map Current Location: This feature allows you to track, within the accuracy of the GPS signal, the location of your phone. You need access the website of the company with which you arranged to provide this service, and it will show you (on a map) the rough location of your phone.

Wipe Your Device Clean

As a last-ditch option, you can use *mobile management software (MMS)*. MMS can remotely disable your device or wipe it clean. Here are some of the possible scenarios:

✔ *You were robbed, and a thief has your phone.*

Remote Lock: After your phone has been taken, this app allows you to create a four-digit PIN that, when sent to your phone from another cellular phone or a web page, locks down your phone. This capability is above and beyond the protection you get from your screen lock, and prevents further access to applications, phone, and data.

If you know that your phone was stolen — that is, not just lost — do *not* try to track down the thief yourself. Get the police involved. Let them know that you have this service on your phone and that you know where your phone is.

✔ *You're a high-level executive or international spy. You stored important plans on your phone, and you have reason to believe that the "other side" has stolen your phone to acquire your secrets.*

Remote Erase: Also known as Remote Wipe, this option resets the phone to its factory settings, wiping out all the information and settings on your phone.

You can't add Remote Erase *after* you've lost your phone. You must sign up for this kind of service beforehand. It's not possible to remotely download the application to your phone. You need to have your phone in hand when you download and install either a lock app or a wipe app.

Put Your Contact Number on the Screensaver

If you've ever found a lost phone, you may recall being faced with a dilemma. Do you

  a. Take it to the local Lost and Found?

  b. Take it to a local carrier?

  c. Try to track down the rightful owner?

  d. Ignore it and not get involved?

Kudos if you do a, b, or c. If you chose c, you hope that the owner has not locked the screen. If you chose b, the store hopes that the screen isn't locked, in which case someone can look at phone calls and texts to contact the owner.

If your phone is the lost one and its screen is locked (as I hope yours is), this plan falls apart — unless you've cleverly put your contact information on the screen. That makes it easy to contact you.

Don't use your cellular phone number as your contact number. I hope I do not have to explain why.

Here are the steps to put your contact information on your lock screen:

1. **From the apps screen, tap the settings icon.**

2. **Tap Lock Screen.**

   This brings up the options shown in Figure 17-7.

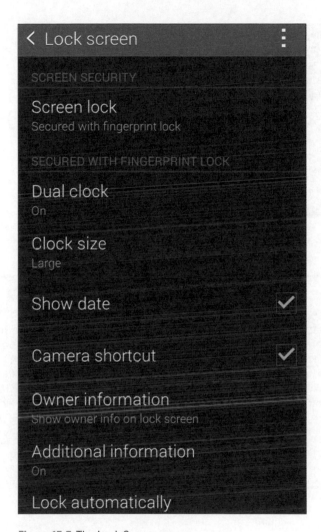

Figure 17-7: The Lock Screen screen.

3. **Tap Owner Information.**

   You can see the screen in Figure 17-8.

4. **Enter an alternative number if the phone is found.**

   This could be a home or work number or an email address. You don't have much space.

   You're all set: The lock screen will display your contact info to whoever finds your phone. Fewer people are likely to handle your phone.

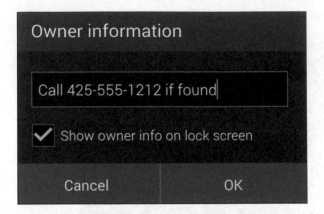

Figure 17-8: The Owner Information screen.

Not I

Before you think that you'll never lose your phone, I should point out some research from the firm In-Stat on this subject. They surveyed a panel of more than 2,000 cellular phone users about how often their phones had been lost or stolen: 64 percent had lost their phones at least once, yet 99 percent of those respondents believed that they were better than average at keeping track of their phones.

These results show that almost all of us think we are pretty good at keeping track of our phones. This same survey found that the respondents lost a phone (on average) every four years. With about 320 million phones in use across the United States, that means more than 200,000 phones sprout legs and walk away on a daily basis.

Make it easy to get your phone back. Make your contact information accessible.

Ten Features to Look for Down the Road

*W*ith the power of your HTC One and the flexibility offered in Android applications development, it can be difficult to imagine that even more capabilities could be in the works. In spite of this, the following are ten features that would improve the usability and value of your HTC One phone.

Fill 'Er Up — Wirelessly

Connecting the micro-USB cable to your HTC One to charge it isn't that big a deal. On the other hand, it could be easier. These days the technology exists to make that connection easier. You can charge your phone wirelessly by putting it on a special mat, for instance, and the charge flows wirelessly into your phone.

Several companies make wireless charging solutions. In addition, the Wireless Power Consortium offers Qi — a standard for wireless charging. The idea is that multiple manufacturers would make Qi-compliant charging mats that would power Qi-compliant phones, regardless of manufacturer.

Your HTC One is not Qi-compliant. Some say that the metal housing is to blame. However, other companies have figured out how to do it. This would be a nice capability to have.

Smarter Customer Care for Your Phone

You may not realize this, but your cellular carrier lives on pins and needles during the first few weeks after you get your new phone. This is the period when you can return your phone, no questions asked. Once you go past that date, you can't cancel your contract without a lot of hassle on your part.

This is why, if you bring your phone back to the store reporting a problem, your carrier will tend to swap out your old phone for a brand new one.

Usually you'll just take the new phone and walk out with a big smile on your face. This outcome is good customer care for most products — but not necessarily good customer care for smartphones. The reason? One of the most common sources of trouble has nothing to do with the phone at all: The customer isn't using it right.

For example, you may have left your Wi-Fi and Bluetooth on all the time, causing your battery to drain too fast. You may have left your phone on your dashboard and cooked the battery. Or, through no fault of your own, you may have downloaded two badly written apps that conflict with each other. The problem here is that unless someone spends the time to help you with the underlying problem, you'll be back in the store with the same problem.

At that point, however, you cannot return your phone. If you're sympathetic, or very annoying, your carrier may give you a refurbished phone. You walk out of the store, but without the biggest smile on your face. Unfortunately, nobody dealt with the underlying trouble, so you'll be back, once again, with the same problem.

No surprise if you start to think that the problem is with that darn phone. In fact, the store needs to listen to you about how you're using the phone and then help you get the most out of it. This is hard to do in a retail environment where the sales people are under pressure to sell lines of service and get no concrete reward for helping you with your problem.

This is where smarter customer care comes in. With the proper tools, you can work with a product expert to troubleshoot your phone. Some companies specialize in understanding the underlying problems and coming up with solutions for consumers. This kind of customer care costs the carriers a little more, but it makes for fewer unnecessary returns of perfectly good phones — and for much happier customers.

Control of Other Home Electronics

You can use your HTC to control your TV. That is good start. Now how about the other electronics in your home?

Traditional home appliances are getting smarter. A problem they have is that adding rows of buttons (so you can control those new capabilities) complicates manufacture. So the next generation of appliances has begun to add a small LCD screen to the appliance. This can look slick, but it costs a lot and is prone to breakage. Also, the fancy capabilities involve pushing a confusing combination of buttons with cryptic messages displayed on a tiny screen.

The latest idea is to omit the screen altogether, and to give you control of the settings through an application on your smartphone. Your appliance keeps the basic buttons, but lets you use the fancy capabilities by setting them through your phone. You would just download the free application made by the manufacturer from the Google Play Store, and have your beautiful and logical user interface to control your new product. No strings attached.

For example, you could turn on your new oven and set the temperature without using a smartphone. However, if you want it to start preheating at 5:30 so you can put in the casserole when you walk in the door, you set that up through your phone.

Many of us have such capabilities on our ovens. In practice, however, features that aren't used regularly don't become intuitive — and finding the instruction manual is often too much of a hassle. An application written on your HTC One, on the other hand, can be very intuitive. In just a few clicks, the oven temperature will be ready when you walk in the door.

Before too long, such capabilities will be available on your washing machine, dryer, security system, sprinklers, thermostat, or refrigerator — all coming soon to an appliance store near you!

Entertainment Selector

The traditional view is that we sit in front of our TVs when we want to be entertained and we sit at our PCs when we want to do something productive or communicate electronically. These clear distinctions have blurred since it became possible to watch movies and TV on a PC.

Now that you have HD resolution on your phone, it's not unreasonable to use your phone to do some channel surfing. When you find what you want, and if it's convenient, you switch to the big-screen TV.

Although such a scenario has been technologically possible in the past, the extreme resolution of your phone makes it convenient and a viable alternative to firing up the big-screen TV in another part of the house.

Existing technology could make this a reality. However, it's not nearly as convenient as it could be. Today, you need to open the right applications or select the right channels. It would be convenient if your phone communicated with the TV and so it would find the right program, and vice versa. It would be slick if the phone watched your eyes and detected when you have taken them off the TV screen, just as it can when you take your eyes off the phone screen.

Information Finder

Your smartphone, which is turned on all the time, is very handy if you need to know the location of the 1994 Winter Olympic Games or the title of Virginia Madsen's first movie. (By the way, it's Lillehammer, Norway and the 1983 movie *Class*.)

On the other hand, if you want to write a research report on the relative merits of a flat tax compared to a value-added tax, you're probably better off working on a PC. This latter project is best done with a full keyboard and large screen. The time to turn on the PC, watch it boot up, sign in, and connect with the Internet is small when compared to the time spent doing the research and writing.

In between these extremes, your phone is becoming the preferred tool for accessing information. The screen, the convenience of the search tools, and the apps all contribute to your phone being the primary source of daily information in lieu of your PC.

 What this means to you is that your investment in your next PC should take into account how you use your smartphone. You may need less PC, depending on your information-collection habits.

More and Better Health Sensors

Chapter 16 mentions the health and fitness sensors that are on the market. Currently, you can get devices that track a single function, such as heartbeat or the oxygen level in your blood. These sensors are just the beginning.

A factor that helps drive this market is the number of smartphone users. It has been growing like gangbusters over the past few years. The number of smartphones sold exceeded the number of dumb phones as of 2012 and shows no sign of slowing. Phones without health sensors are now the exception rather than the rule.

Finally, these devices have the potential to improve your health. It won't be too long before first responders can have the information to render better services faster because they'll know many of the patient's vital signs (via smartphone) before they even leave the station.

Better 911 Services

The 911 system has been helping the U.S. for more than 45 years. The dirty secret of this service is that the technology that gives the caller's location hasn't been updated in a long time.

To put this in perspective, your smartphone is designed to work with data at up to 300 *million* bits per second. When you call 911, the phone that answers your call is designed to work with data at up to 120 *bits* per second. (Seriously. I am not making this up.)

Many states and regions are trying to address this problem. This effort is called *next-generation 911* or *NG911*. NG911 promises to make the information you already have on your phone available to the people who are sending you help. This new technology is slowly being implemented region by region in different states and counties.

For example, most 911 dispatchers can't access the data from the health sensors described in the previous section. With NG911, you can set up your phone so that first responders get your vital signs and EKG the moment they get the call.

With a larger data pipeline between your smartphone and the first responders, you can send anything that's relevant, including medical history, your emergency contacts, insurance data, and whether you have any protection orders against stalkers. All this information can help you — and it's available right away because regardless of where you happen to be, your phone is typically there with you.

Simpler Bluetooth Pairing

Paring with Bluetooth devices is pretty darn simple. It would be nice if it were even simpler.

Having the application handle all the settings. Downloading an app is easy from Google Play Store. All Bluetooth devices come with an app that helps you set up, even if all the app does is handle the pairing.

More Body English/Less Tapping

Tapping is easy, but tilting or twisting your screen can be a more natural motion. For example, Nintendo shook up the gaming world back in 2006 when it launched the Wii gaming console with the Wii remote. The Wii remote added an accelerometer, which opened up a new gaming experience by letting the game player communicate with the game through motion.

Well, guess what: Your HTC One has a very accurate accelerometer that can also tell the game what to do with the bowling ball, tennis racket, or whatever.

Up to now, very few applications or games have taken advantage of this capability. All the elements are there in the device to enable it to interpret gestures. The apps just need to take advantage of those elements.

Serving You Better

The smartphone is what companies use to find a better way to serve you. This will show up in a few ways.

The first is in much better mobile advertising. There has long been talk that advertisers can tell where you are and then provide ads or coupons based on your proximity. This is starting to become a reality, though it's still kinda clumsy. If you have been Googling, say, televisions, you may see ads relating to sales about televisions.

In the future, however, your phone may tell you about a sale going on for televisions when you walk by the Sears store in the mall. That is cool. Even cooler is to be told that that particular model is on sale at the Sears store and that this particular sale is the best in town by over $20. This can happen if you are doing research at the moment. It may be possible for your app to flag you if you have already researched this on the Internet.

The second way smartphones are enhancing service is by automating the order-taking process. For example, wherever you see a video kiosk, that company can allow you to interact with the kiosk via your HTC One. Some fast-food restaurants have installed kiosks so that customers can bypass the line to order from the menu. The items are totaled and paid for by credit card. The customer steps aside and waits for the order.

This exact transaction could take place on your smartphone. You don't have to wait while the joker in front of you decides between a double cheeseburger or two single cheeseburgers . . . and hold the pickles. Instead, you can place your order on your smartphone and wait with eager anticipation to find out what toys are in your kid's meal.

Index

• F •

• G •

● *H* ●

About the Author

Bill Hughes is an experienced marketing strategy executive with over two decades of experience in sales, strategic marketing, and business development roles at several leading corporations, including Microsoft, IBM, General Electric, Motorola, and US West Cellular.

Dedication

I would like to dedicate this book to my son, Quinlan, as he begins his future as an Eagle Scout.

Author's Acknowledgments

I need to thank a number of people who helped make this book a reality. First, I would thank my literary agent, Carole Jelen, of Waterside Publishing, for her support, encouragement, knowledge, and negotiation skills.

I would also like to thank the team at Wiley Publishing: Katie Mohr and Tonya Cupp. Your expertise helped me through the creative process. Thanks for your guidance.

I would like to thank Thomas Chun and Josh Mason of Samsung Telecommunications America for their assistance.

I would like to acknowledge my son, Quinlan, for keeping it relatively quiet (other than throwing the ball for Indy which bounced off my office door too many times) as I wrote this book. I would like to Arlen for successfully negotiating freshman year at WSU and Ellis for graduating with his degree in bioengineering.

Finally, I need to acknowledge the support and patience of my wife, Susan, as I wrote this book.

Publisher's Acknowledgments

Senior Acquisitions Editor: Katie Mohr

Project Editor: Tonya Maddox Cupp

Editorial Assistant: Claire Johnson

Sr. Editorial Assistant: Cherie Case

Project Coordinator: Lauren Buroker

Cover Image: © 2014 HTC Corporation. All rights reserved. Used by permission.

Apple & Mac

iPad For Dummies,
6th Edition
978-1-118-72306-7

iPhone For Dummies,
7th Edition
978-1-118-69083-3

Macs All-in-One
For Dummies, 4th Edition
978-1-118-82210-4

OS X Mavericks
For Dummies
978-1-118-69188-5

Blogging & Social Media

Facebook For Dummies,
5th Edition
978-1-118-63312-0

Social Media Engagement
For Dummies
978-1-118-53019-1

WordPress For Dummies,
6th Edition
978-1-118-79161-5

Business

Stock Investing
For Dummies, 4th Edition
978-1-118-37678-2

Investing For Dummies,
6th Edition
978-0-470-90545-6

Personal Finance
For Dummies, 7th Edition
978-1-118-11785-9

QuickBooks 2014
For Dummies
978-1-118-72005-9

Small Business Marketing
Kit For Dummies,
3rd Edition
978-1-118-31183-7

Careers

Job Interviews
For Dummies, 4th Edition
978-1-118-11290-8

Job Searching with Social
Media For Dummies,
2nd Edition
978-1-118-67856-5

Personal Branding
For Dummies
978-1-118-11792-7

Resumes For Dummies,
6th Edition
978-0-470-87361-8

Starting an Etsy Business
For Dummies, 2nd Edition
978-1-118-59024-9

Diet & Nutrition

Belly Fat Diet For Dummies
978-1-118-34585-6

Mediterranean Diet
For Dummies
978-1-118-71525-3

Nutrition For Dummies,
5th Edition
978-0-470-93231-5

Digital Photography

Digital SLR Photography
All-in-One For Dummies,
2nd Edition
978-1-118-59082-9

Digital SLR Video &
Filmmaking For Dummies
978-1-118-36598-4

Photoshop Elements 12
For Dummies
978-1-118-72714-0

Gardening

Herb Gardening
For Dummies, 2nd Edition
978-0-470-61778-6

Gardening with Free-Range
Chickens For Dummies
978-1-118-54754-0

Health

Boosting Your Immunity
For Dummies
978-1-118-40200-9

Diabetes For Dummies,
4th Edition
978-1-118-29447-5

Living Paleo For Dummies
978-1-118-29405-5

Big Data

Big Data For Dummies
978-1-118-50422-2

Data Visualization
For Dummies
978-1-118-50289-1

Hadoop For Dummies
978-1-118-60755-8

Language &
Foreign Language

500 Spanish Verbs
For Dummies
978-1-118-02382-2

English Grammar
For Dummies, 2nd Edition
978-0-470-54664-2

French All-in-One
For Dummies
978-1-118-22815-9

German Essentials
For Dummies
978-1-118-18422-6

Italian For Dummies,
2nd Edition
978-1-118-00465-4

e Available in print and eBook formats.

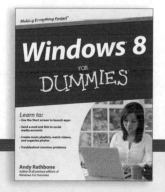

Available wherever books are sold. **For more information or to order direct visit www.dummies.com**

Math & Science

Algebra I For Dummies,
2nd Edition
978-0-470-55964-2

Anatomy and Physiology
For Dummies, 2nd Edition
978-0-470-92326-9

Astronomy For Dummies,
3rd Edition
978-1-118-37697-3

Biology For Dummies,
2nd Edition
978-0-470-59875-7

Chemistry For Dummies,
2nd Edition
978-1-118-00730-3

1001 Algebra II Practice
Problems For Dummies
978-1-118-44662-1

Microsoft Office

Excel 2013 For Dummies
978-1-118-51012-4

Office 2013 All-in-One
For Dummies
978-1-118-51636-2

PowerPoint 2013
For Dummies
978-1-118-50253-2

Word 2013 For Dummies
978-1-118-49123-2

Music

Blues Harmonica
For Dummies
978-1-118-25269-7

Guitar For Dummies,
3rd Edition
978-1-118-11554-1

iPod & iTunes
For Dummies, 10th Edition
978-1-118-50864-0

Programming

Beginning Programming
with C For Dummies
978-1-118-73763-7

Excel VBA Programming
For Dummies, 3rd Edition
978-1-118-49037-2

Java For Dummies,
6th Edition
978-1-118-40780-6

Religion & Inspiration

The Bible For Dummies
978-0-7645-5296-0

Buddhism For Dummies,
2nd Edition
978-1-118-02379-2

Catholicism For Dummies,
2nd Edition
978-1-118-07778-8

Self-Help & Relationships

Beating Sugar Addiction
For Dummies
978-1-118-54645-1

Meditation For Dummies,
3rd Edition
978-1-118-29144-3

Seniors

Laptops For Seniors
For Dummies, 3rd Edition
978-1-118-71105-7

Computers For Seniors
For Dummies, 3rd Edition
978-1-118-11553-4

iPad For Seniors
For Dummies, 6th Edition
978-1-118-72826-0

Social Security
For Dummies
978-1-118-20573-0

Smartphones & Tablets

Android Phones
For Dummies, 2nd Edition
978-1-118-72030-1

Nexus Tablets
For Dummies
978-1-118-77243-0

Samsung Galaxy S 4
For Dummies
978-1-118-64222-1

Samsung Galaxy Tabs
For Dummies
978-1-118-77294-2

Test Prep

ACT For Dummies,
5th Edition
978-1-118-01259-8

ASVAB For Dummies,
3rd Edition
978-0-470-63760-9

GRE For Dummies,
7th Edition
978-0-470-88921-3

Officer Candidate Tests
For Dummies
978-0-470-59876-4

Physician's Assistant Exam
For Dummies
978-1-118-11556-5

Series 7 Exam For Dummies
978-0-470-09932-2

Windows 8

Windows 8.1 All-in-One
For Dummies
978-1-118-82087-2

Windows 8.1 For Dummies
978-1-118-82121-3

Windows 8.1 For Dummies,
Book + DVD Bundle
978-1-118-82107-7

📖 Available in print and eBook formats.

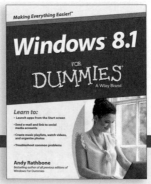

Available wherever books are sold. **For more information or to order direct visit www.dummies.com**

Take Dummies with you everywhere you go!

Whether you are excited about eBooks, want more from the web, must have your mobile apps, or are swept up in social media, Dummies makes everything easier.

Visit Us

bit.ly/JE0O

Like Us

on.fb.me/1f1ThNu

Follow Us

bit.ly/ZDytkR

Watch Us

bit.ly/gbOQHn

Join Us

linkd.in/1gurkMm

Pin Us

bit.ly/16caOLd

Circle Us

bit.ly/1aQTuDQ

Shop Us

bit.ly/4dEp9

Leverage the Power

For Dummies is the global leader in the reference category and one of the most trusted and highly regarded brands in the world. No longer just focused on books, customers now have access to the For Dummies content they need in the format they want. Let us help you develop a solution that will fit your brand and help you connect with your customers.

Advertising & Sponsorships

Connect with an engaged audience on a powerful multimedia site, and position your message alongside expert how-to content.

Targeted ads • Video • Email marketing • Microsites • Sweepstakes sponsorship

21 Million Monthly Page Views & 13 Million Unique Visitors

Custom Publishing

Reach a global audience in any language by creating a solution that will differentiate you from competitors, amplify your message, and encourage customers to make a buying decision.

Apps • Books • eBooks • Video • Audio • Webinars

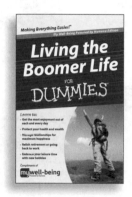   

Brand Licensing & Content

Leverage the strength of the world's most popular reference brand to reach new audiences and channels of distribution.

For more information, visit www.Dummies.com/biz

Dummies products make life easier!

- DIY
- Consumer Electronics
- Crafts
- Software
- Cookware
- Hobbies
- Videos
- Music
- Games
- and More!

For more information, go to **Dummies.com** and search the store by category.

FOR
DUMMIES

A Wiley Brand